Families That Care and Share

SIGNATURES

Senior Authors
Roger C. Farr
Dorothy S. Strickland

Authors
Richard F. Abrahamson ♦ Alma Flor Ada ♦ Barbara Bowen Coulter
Bernice E. Cullinan ♦ Margaret A. Gallego
W. Dorsey Hammond
Nancy Roser ♦ Junko Yokota ♦ Hallie Kay Yopp

Senior Consultant
Asa G. Hilliard III

Consultants
V. Kanani Choy ♦ Lee Bennett Hopkins ♦ Stephen Krashen ♦ Rosalia Salinas

Harcourt Brace & Company
Orlando Atlanta Austin Boston San Francisco Chicago Dallas New York Toronto London

Copyright © 1997 by Harcourt Brace & Company. All rights reserved. ISBN 0-15-308316-6
2 3 4 5 6 7 8 9 10   048   99 98 97

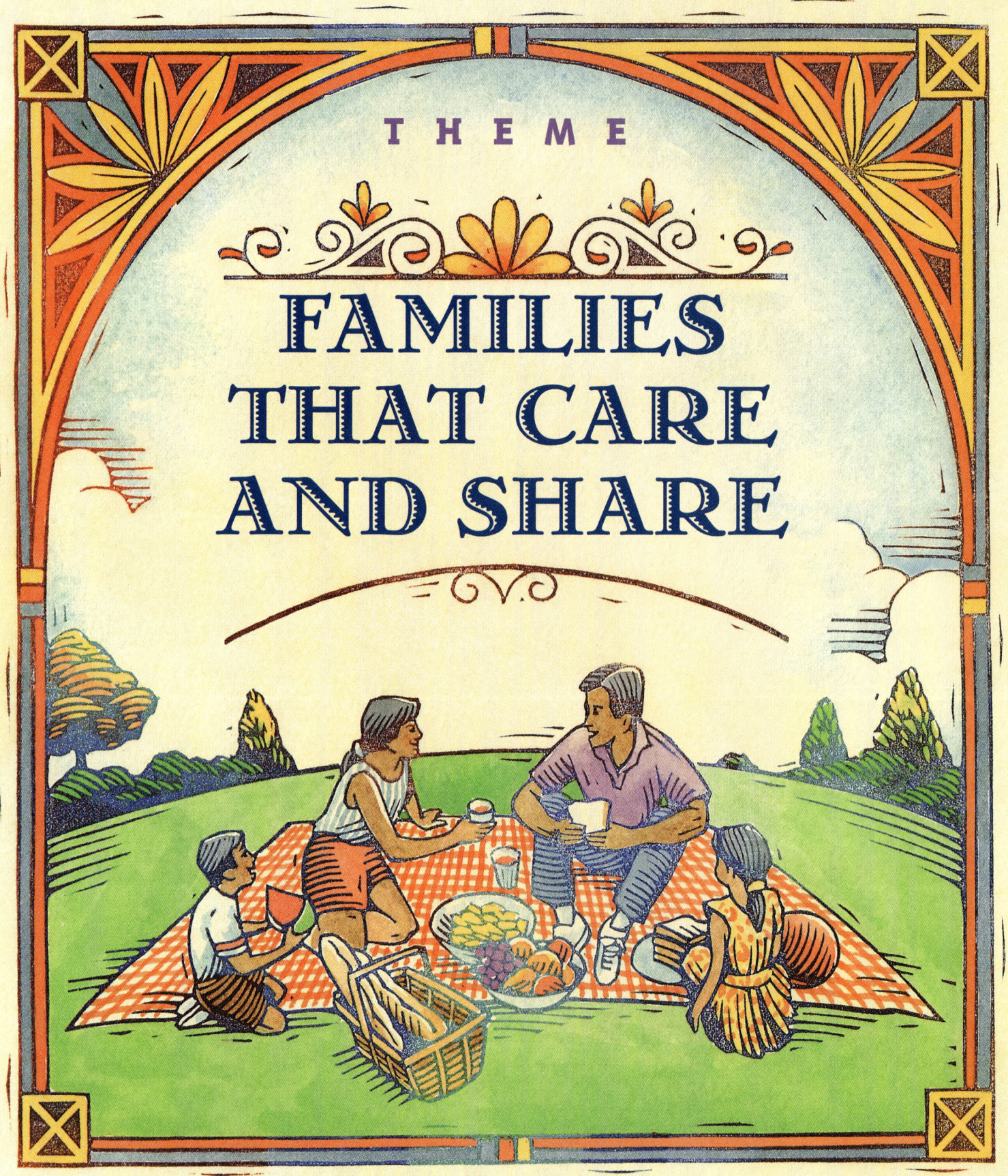

CONTENTS

13 Theme Opener

16 Bookshelf

Cumulative Tale/Social Studies
18 Shoes from Grandpa
by Mem Fox
illustrated by Patricia Mullins

    Author and Illustrator Features:
    Mem Fox and Patricia Mullins

Realistic Fiction/Social Studies
46 The Relatives Came
by Cynthia Rylant
illustrated by Stephen Gammell

    Author and Illustrator Features:
    Cynthia Rylant and Stephen Gammell

Poem
62 Families, Families
by Dorothy and Michael Strickland

How-to Article/Social Studies
66 Family Treasure Chest
by Scott Bricher
from *Kid City*

Art
68 Art and Literature: Making Tamales
by Carmen Lomas Garza

Realistic Fiction/Social Studies
70 Too Many Tamales
by Gary Soto
illustrated by Ed Martinez

    Author and Illustrator Features:
    Gary Soto and Ed Martinez

Recipes/Social Studies
94 A World of Treats!

Realistic Fiction/Social Studies
100 Willie's Not the Hugging Kind
by Joyce Durham Barrett
illustrated by Pat Cummings

    Author and Illustrator Features:
    Joyce Durham Barrett and Pat Cummings

120 Theme Wrap-Up

349 Glossary

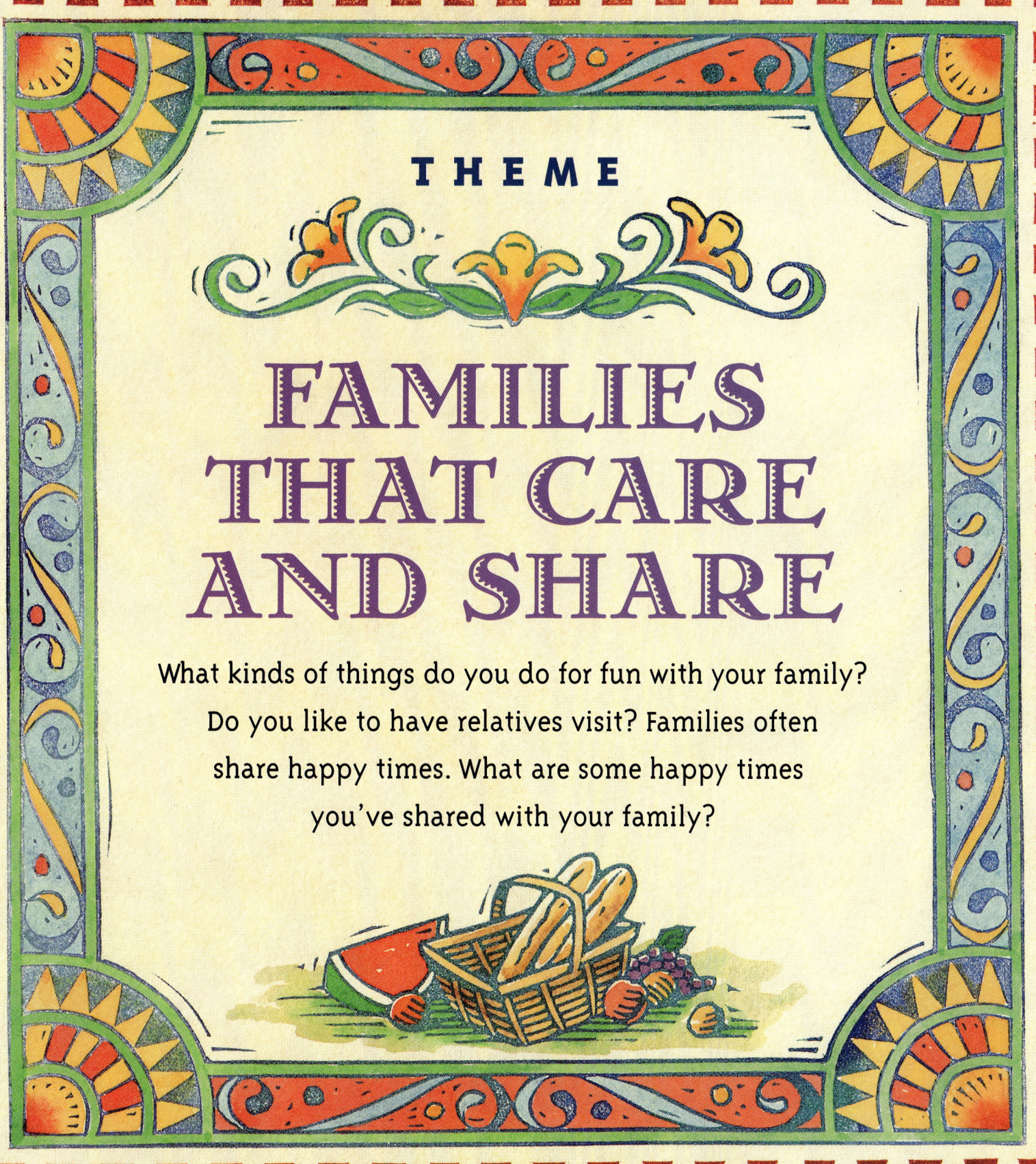

THEME

FAMILIES THAT CARE AND SHARE

What kinds of things do you do for fun with your family? Do you like to have relatives visit? Families often share happy times. What are some happy times you've shared with your family?

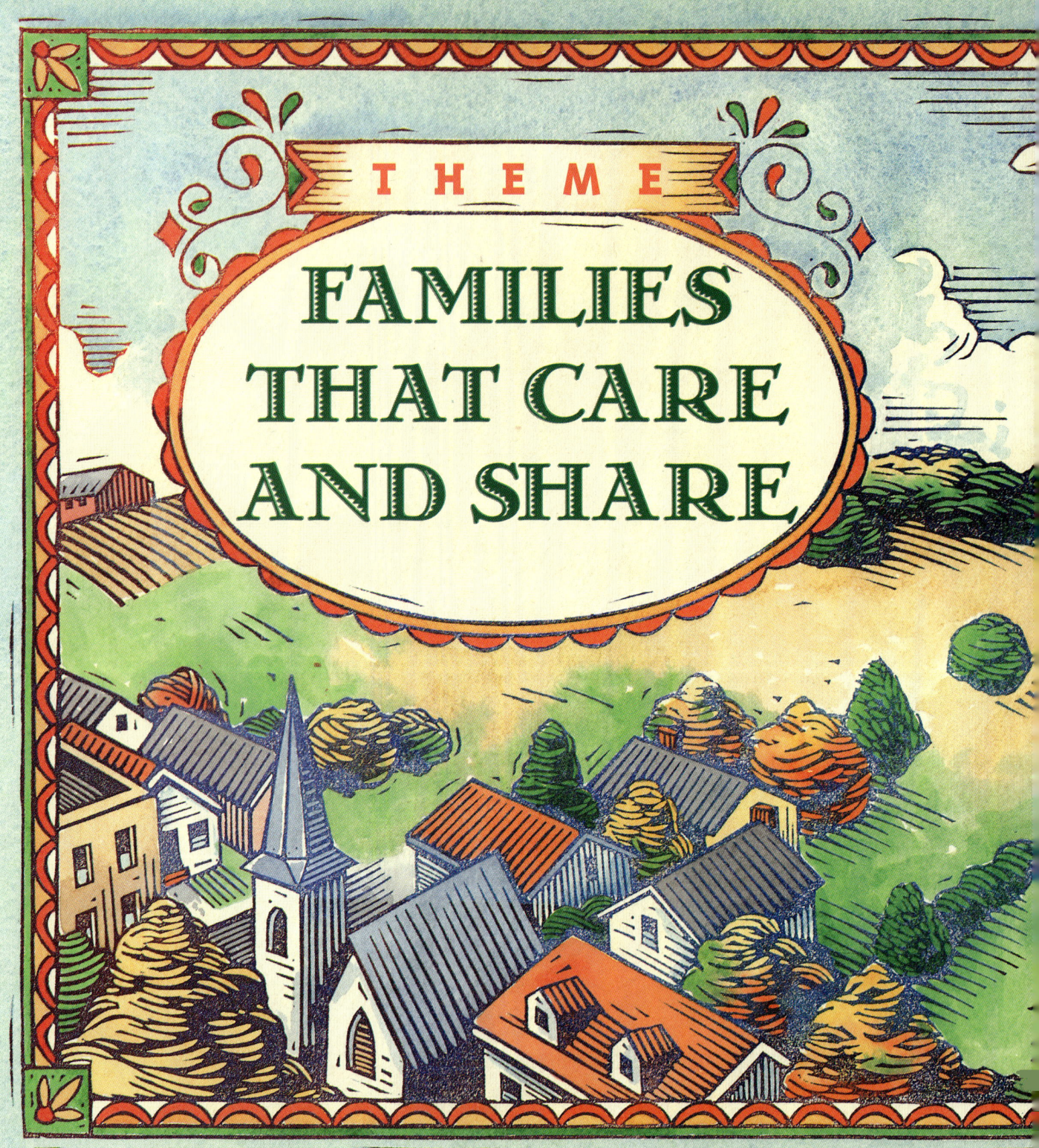

CONTENTS

SHOES FROM GRANDPA
by Mem Fox

THE RELATIVES CAME
by Cynthia Rylant

FAMILIES, FAMILIES
by Dorothy and Michael Strickland

FAMILY TREASURE CHEST
by Scott Bricher

ART AND LITERATURE:
Making Tamales
by Carmen Lomas Garza

TOO MANY TAMALES
by Gary Soto

A WORLD OF TREATS!

WILLIE'S NOT THE HUGGING KIND
by Joyce Durham Barrett

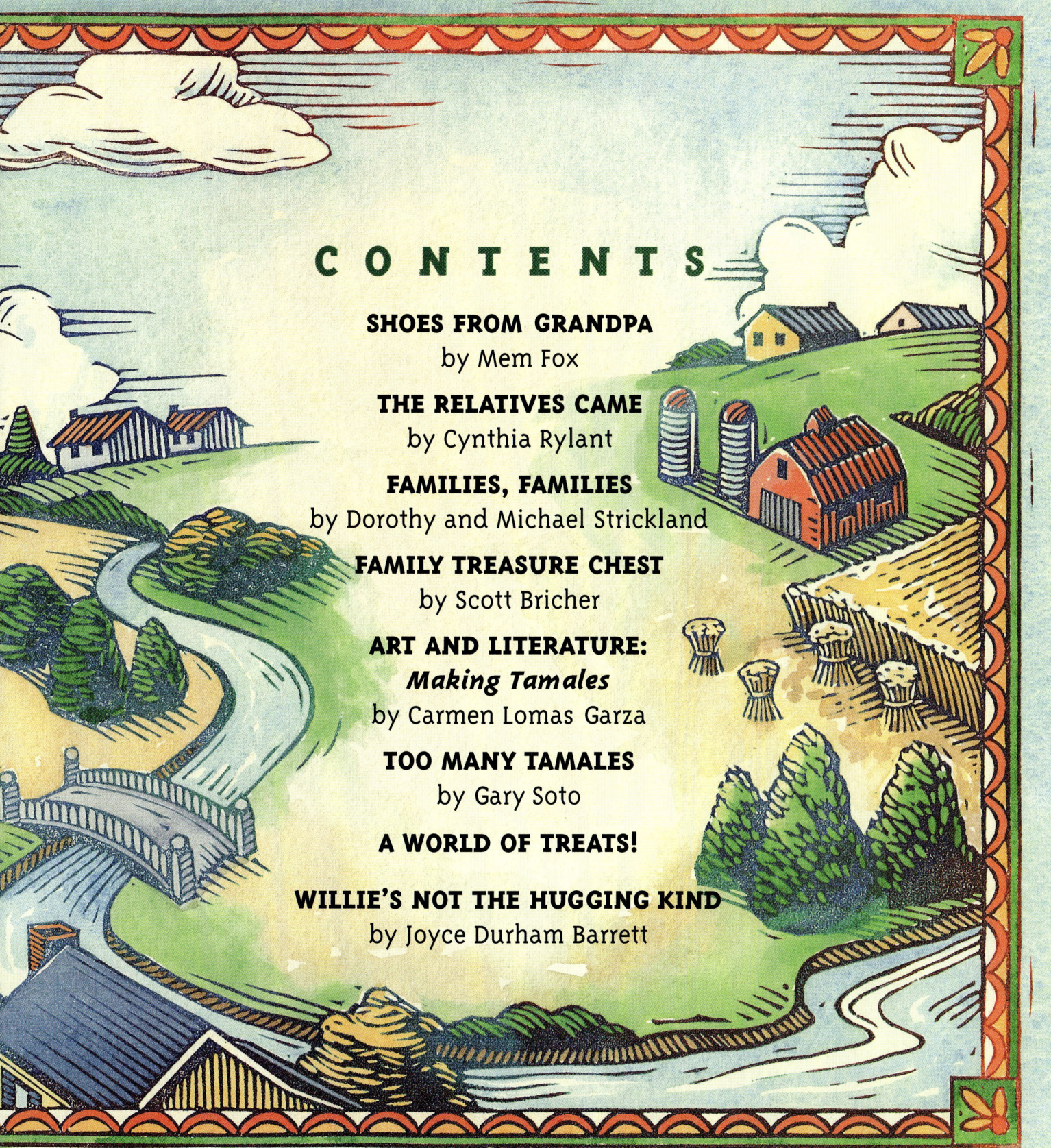

BOOKSHELF

Who's Who in My Family?
written and illustrated
by Loreen Leedy

Join Ms. Fox's class and find out how each person in your family is related to you.
Signatures Library
Award-Winning Author

JoJo's Flying Side Kick
written and illustrated
by Brian Pinkney

Will JoJo pass the test in her Tae Kwon Do class? How does her family help her?
Signatures Library
Award-Winning Author

At the Beach
by Huy Voun Lee

A mother teaches her son to write in Chinese while they spend a day at the beach.

A Birthday Basket for Tía
by Pat Mora

Cecilia finds the perfect gift for her great-aunt's birthday.
Award-Winning Author

Tomorrow on Rocky Pond
by Lynn Reiser

A family looks forward to a fishing trip at Rocky Pond.
Children's Choice

Late one summer Jessie's father invited all the family over for a barbecue.

When Grandpa saw Jessie he stood back and said, "My, how you've grown! You'll need a new pair of shoes this winter, and I'll buy them."

"Thanks a lot, Grandpa," said Jessie.

Then her dad said,
"I'll buy you some socks from the local shops,
to go with the shoes from Grandpa."

And her mom said,
"I'll buy you a skirt that won't show the dirt,
to go with the socks from the local shops,
to go with the shoes from Grandpa."

And her cousin said,
"I'll look for a blouse with ribbons and bows,
to go with the skirt that won't show the dirt,
to go with the socks from the local shops,
to go with the shoes from Grandpa."

And her sister said,
"I'll get you a sweater when the weather gets wetter,
to go with the blouse with ribbons and bows,
to go with the skirt that won't show the dirt,
to go with the socks from the local shops,
to go with the shoes from Grandpa."

And her grandma said,
"I'll find you a coat you could wear on a boat,
to go with the sweater when the weather gets wetter,
to go with the blouse with ribbons and bows,
to go with the skirt that won't show the dirt,
to go with the socks from the local shops,
to go with the shoes from Grandpa."

And her aunt said,
"I'll knit you a scarf that'll make us all laugh,
to go with the coat you could wear on a boat,
to go with the sweater when the weather gets wetter,
to go with the blouse with ribbons and bows,

to go with the skirt that won't show the dirt,
to go with the socks from the local shops,
to go with the shoes from Grandpa."

And her brother said,
"I'll find you a hat you can put on like that,
to go with the scarf that'll make us all laugh,
to go with the coat you could wear on a boat,
to go with the sweater when the weather gets wetter,
to go with the blouse with ribbons and bows,

to go with the skirt that won't show the dirt,
to go with the socks from the local shops,
to go with the shoes from Grandpa."

And her uncle said,
"I'll buy you some mittens that are softer than kittens,
to go with the hat you can put on like that,
to go with the scarf that'll make us all laugh,
to go with the coat you could wear on a boat,

to go with the sweater when the weather gets wetter,
to go with the blouse with ribbons and bows,
to go with the skirt that won't show the dirt,
to go with the socks from the local shops,
to go with the shoes from Grandpa."

And Jessie said,
"You're all so kind that I hate to be mean,
but please, would one of you buy me some jeans?"

MEM FOX

Mem Fox was born in Australia, but she grew up in Africa. She loved to climb trees, ride bikes, and play football. She also loved to read and write. She wrote her first story when she was ten years old.

Now, she writes books for children because she wants *you* to enjoy reading. Her ideas come from things that happened in her life.

PATRICIA MULLINS

Art was Patricia Mullins's favorite subject in school. She especially liked drawing animals. She liked making animals from paper, cloth scraps, or anything she could find. She also enjoyed going to puppet shows. Can you find puppets in the story?

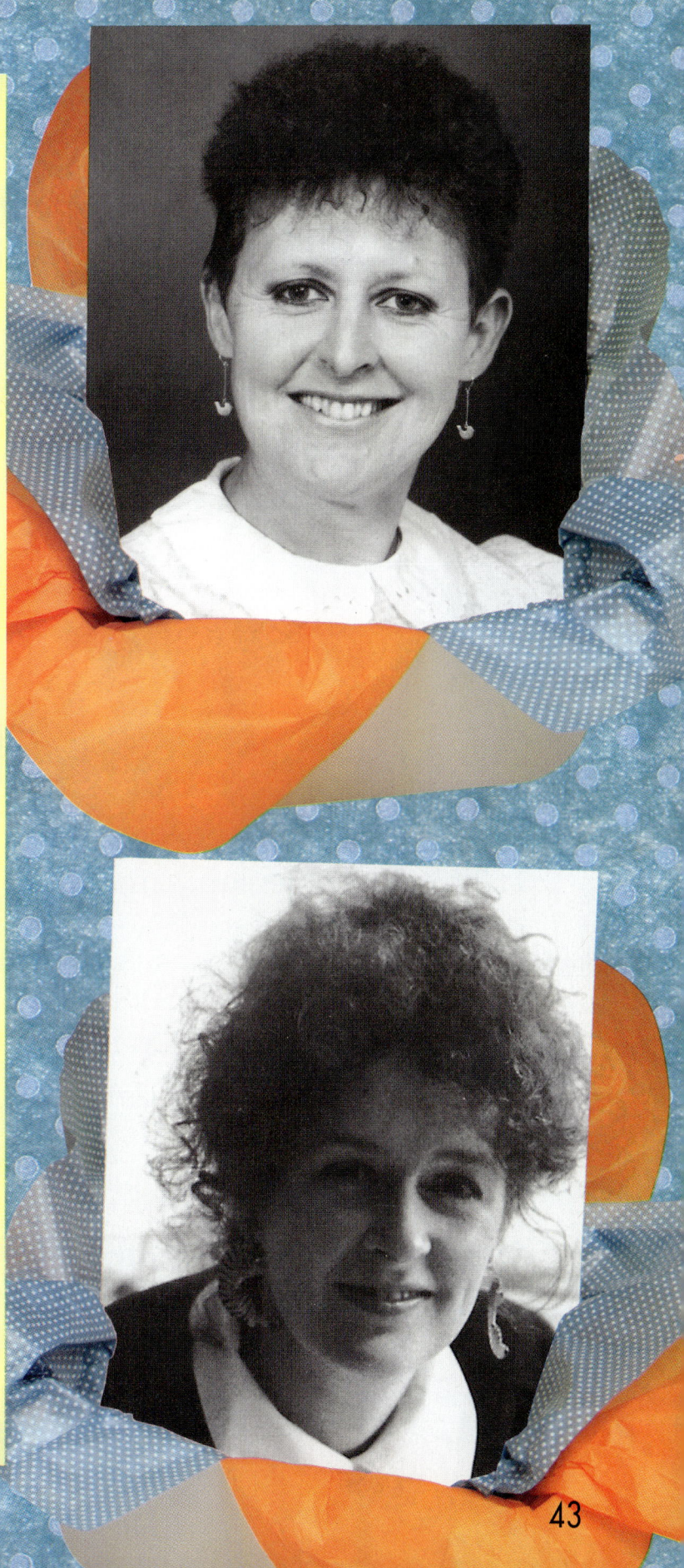

Response

MAKE A COLLAGE

RIP IT UP

For *Shoes from Grandpa,* Patricia Mullins made collages from torn paper and bits of cloth. You can make a collage, too!

You will need:
construction paper
glue
feathers, yarn, buttons, cloth, and other small objects

1. Think of a person, animal, or place.
2. Tear pieces of construction paper. Move them around on a big sheet of paper until you like your picture.
3. Glue the pieces down.
4. Add bits of cloth or other decorations.

One day I walked everywhere. I walked to Joey's house to see the new puppies.

corner

One day I walked everywhere. I walked to Joey's house to see the new puppies. I walked to the corner store to buy some milk.

CREATE A CUMULATIVE TALE
MAKE UP A STORY

Each part of "Shoes from Grandpa" adds something to the part that comes before it. Work with a group to make up a story like that.

1. Decide what your story will be about. Think of a good beginning sentence.
2. One person says that sentence and adds another sentence. Each person repeats the story and adds another part.

WHAT DO YOU THINK?

- How did "Shoes from Grandpa" start? How did it end?
- How do you think Jessie's relatives might answer her question at the end of the story? How would *you* answer her question?

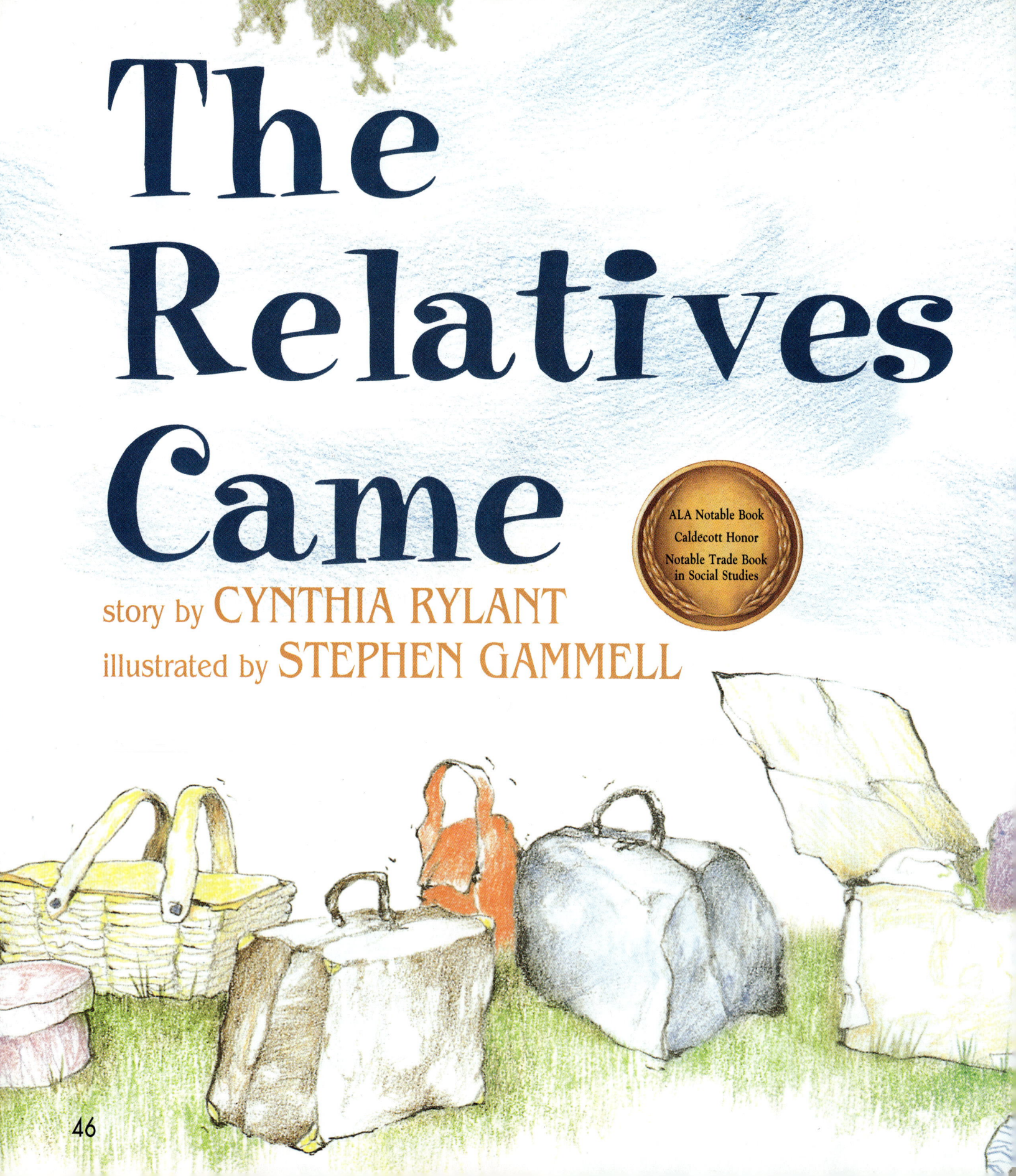

The Relatives Came

story by CYNTHIA RYLANT
illustrated by STEPHEN GAMMELL

ALA Notable Book
Caldecott Honor
Notable Trade Book in Social Studies

It was in the summer of the year when the relatives came. They came up from Virginia. They left when their grapes were nearly purple enough to pick, but not quite.

They had an old station wagon that smelled like a real car, and in it they put an ice chest full of soda pop and some boxes of crackers and some bologna sandwiches, and up they came—from Virginia.

They left at four in the morning when it was still dark, before even the birds were awake.

They drove all day long and into the night, and while they traveled along they looked at the strange houses and different mountains and they thought about their almost purple grapes back home. They thought about Virginia— but they thought about us, too. Waiting for them.

So they drank up all their pop and ate up all their crackers and traveled up all those miles until finally they pulled into our yard.

50

Then it was hugging time. Talk about hugging! Those relatives just passed us all around their car, pulling us against their wrinkled Virginia clothes, crying sometimes. They hugged us for hours.

Then it was into the house and so much laughing and shining faces and hugging in the doorways. You'd have to go through at least four different hugs to get from the kitchen to the front room. Those relatives!

And finally after a big supper two or three times around until we all got a turn at the table, there was quiet talk and we were in twos and threes through the house.

The relatives weren't particular about beds, which was good since there weren't any extras, so a few squeezed in with us and the rest slept on the floor, some with their arms thrown over the closest person, or some with an arm across one person and a leg across another.

It was different, going to sleep with all that new breathing in the house.

The relatives stayed for weeks and weeks. They helped us tend the garden and they fixed any broken things they could find.

They ate up all our strawberries and melons, then promised we could eat up all their grapes and peaches when we came to Virginia.

But none of us thought about Virginia much. We were so busy hugging and eating and breathing together.

Finally, after a long time, the relatives loaded up their ice chest
and headed back to Virginia at four in the morning.
We stood there in our pajamas and waved them off in the dark.
 We watched the relatives disappear down the road,
then we crawled back into our beds that felt too big and too quiet.
We fell asleep.

And the relatives drove on, all day long and into the night, and while they traveled along they looked at the strange houses and different mountains and they thought about their dark purple grapes waiting at home in Virginia.

But they thought about us, too. Missing them. And they missed us.

And when they were finally home in Virginia, they crawled into their silent, soft beds and dreamed about the next summer.

CYNTHIA RYLANT

Sometimes Cynthia Rylant's stories are made-up. Other times, she writes about things that really happened. *The Relatives Came* is a story about the summer that a bunch of relatives came to West Virginia for a visit. They really drove all night from Virginia and stayed for weeks. Aunts, uncles, and cousins fixed broken things, cooked and ate together, and enjoyed each other's company.

Cynthia Rylant doesn't live in West Virginia anymore, but she visits there. She likes to hear the news about the rest of her family from her grandmother. And she likes to eat her mom's corn bread. All the relatives love to see Cynthia and are proud to read her newest books.

Cynthia Rylant

STEPHEN GAMMELL

Look closely at the pictures in this story, and you will see some of *my* relatives. My wife is the photographer. (She really is one!) My dad is cutting hair, and my grandma and grandpa are gardening. Can you find me playing the guitar?

When I drew the pictures for this story, I thought about fun times I had spent with my family when I was young. Did you see the kids playing in boxes? My friends and I used to line up big boxes and then zoom away in our pretend trains and cars. It was fun!

Some of the pictures do not really have words to go along with them. I think that's what makes it fun to look at a story over and over. Every time you do, you can see something new.

Stephen Gammell

Families, Families

FAMILIES, FAMILIES
All kinds of families.
Mommies and daddies,
Sisters and brothers,
Aunties and uncles,
    And cousins, too.

FAMILIES, FAMILIES
All kinds of families.
People who live with us,
People who care for us,
Grandmas and grandpas,
    And babies, brand new.

FAMILIES, FAMILIES
All kinds of families.
Coming and going,
Laughing and singing,
Caring and sharing,
    And loving you.

Dorothy and Michael Strickland
illustration by Brenda Joysmith

Response Corner

CREATE A BROCHURE

Home Away from Home

The relatives in the story traveled a long way. Work with a partner. Pretend you own a hotel. Make up a booklet that tells about your hotel. Tell why your hotel is a good place for travelers who are far from home.

1. Pick a name for your hotel.
2. Plan what you want to say about your hotel. Tell what the rooms are like. Tell about fun things to do there.
3. Write your booklet. Include a drawing of your hotel.

WRITE A LETTER

Dear Relative

Write a letter to one of your relatives or to someone who lives in a place you would like to visit. Tell why you would like to go there. Name things you would like to do when you are there.

What Do You Think?

- What are some things the relatives did during their visit?
- Which would you rather do, go on a visit or have someone visit you? Tell why.

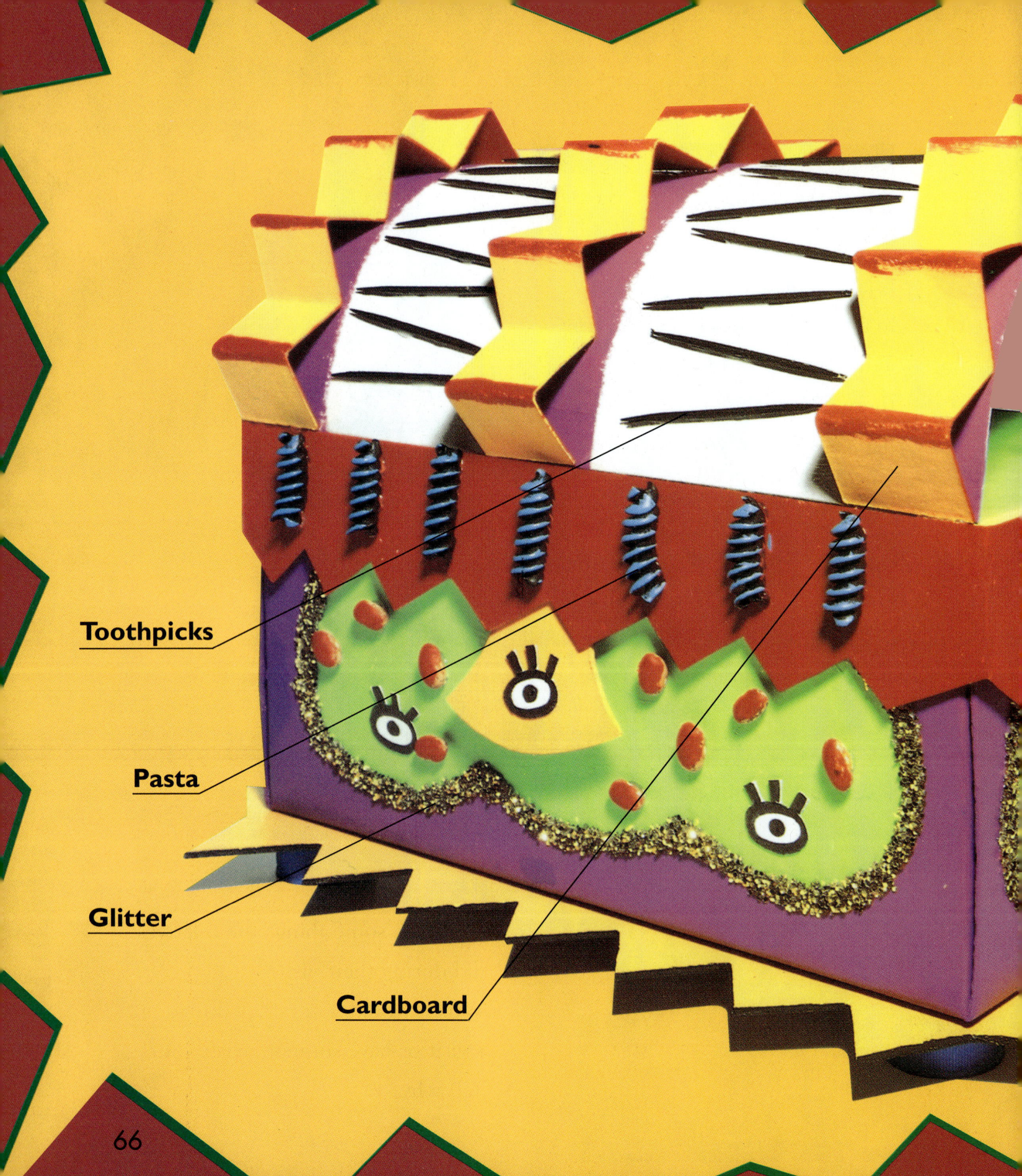

Family Treasure Chest

Pipe Cleaner

Bottle Cap

Beans

Don't Get Rid of That!

Someday you'll be glad you saved that funny photo of your sister, the first baseball card you ever traded, the feather from last year's Halloween costume. Other people might think it's junk, but to you it's family treasure. Make a chest like ours to hold your precious stuff!

ART & LITERATURE

Look at the painting by Carmen Lomas Garza. It shows the artist's family making a food called tamales. How is this family like the families you have read about? The next story you will read is about a family making tamales.

Making Tamales
by Carmen Lomas Garza

Carmen Lomas Garza paints pictures that tell stories about her childhood in Texas. She put herself in this painting. Can you see her standing next to the man in the blue overalls?

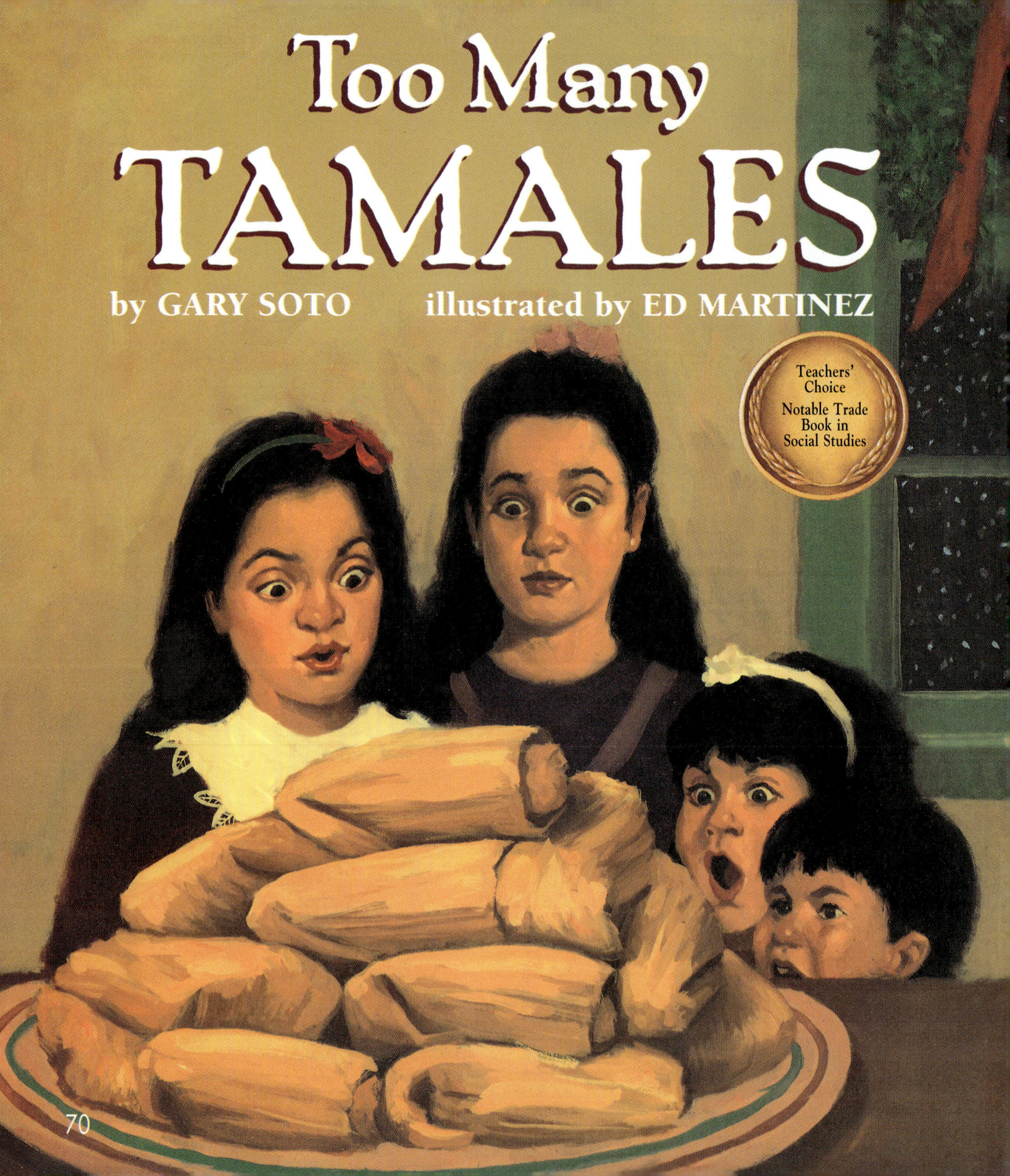

Snow drifted through the streets and now that it was dusk, Christmas trees glittered in the windows.

Maria moved her nose off the glass and came back to the counter. She was acting grown-up now, helping her mother make tamales. Their hands were sticky with *masa*.

"That's very good," her mother said.

Maria happily kneaded the *masa*. She felt grown-up, wearing her mother's apron. Her mom had even let her wear lipstick and perfume. If only I could wear Mom's ring, she thought to herself.

Maria's mother had placed her diamond ring on the kitchen counter. Maria loved that ring. She loved how it sparkled, like their Christmas tree lights.

When her mother left the kitchen to answer the telephone, Maria couldn't help herself. She wiped her hands on the apron and looked back at the door.

"I'll wear the ring for just a minute," she said to herself.

The ring sparkled on her thumb.

Maria returned to kneading the *masa,* her hands pumping up and down. On her thumb the ring disappeared, then reappeared in the sticky glob of dough.

Her mother returned and took the bowl from her. "Go get your father for this part," she said.

 Then the three of them began to spread *masa* onto corn husks. Maria's father helped by plopping a spoonful of meat in the center and folding the husk. He then placed them in a large pot on the stove.
 They made twenty-four tamales as the windows grew white with delicious-smelling curls of steam.

A few hours later the family came over with armfuls of bright presents: her grandparents, her uncle and aunt, and her cousins Dolores, Teresa, and Danny.

Maria kissed everyone hello. Then she grabbed Dolores by the arm and took her upstairs to play, with the other cousins tagging along after them.

They cut out pictures from the newspaper, pictures of toys they were hoping were wrapped and sitting underneath the Christmas tree. As Maria was snipping out a picture of a pearl necklace, a shock spread through her body.

"The ring!" she screamed.

Everyone stared at her. "What ring?" Dolores asked.

Without answering, Maria ran to the kitchen.

The steaming tamales lay piled on a platter. The ring is inside one of the tamales, she thought to herself. It must have come off when I was kneading the *masa*.

Dolores, Teresa, and Danny skidded into the kitchen behind her.

"Help me!" Maria cried.

They looked at each other. Danny piped up first. "What do you want us to do?"

"Eat them," she said. "If you bite something hard, tell me."

The four of them started eating. They ripped off the husks and bit into them. The first one was good, the second one pretty good, but by the third tamale, they were tired of the taste.

"Keep eating," Maria scolded.

Corn husks littered the floor. Their stomachs were stretched till they hurt, but the cousins kept eating until only one tamale remained on the plate.

"This must be it," she said. "The ring must be in that one! We'll each take a bite. You first, Danny."

Danny was the youngest, so he didn't argue. He took a bite. Nothing.

Dolores took a bite. Nothing. Teresa took a big bite. Still nothing. It was Maria's turn. She took a deep breath and slowly, gently, bit into the last mouthful of tamale.

Nothing!

"Didn't any of you bite something hard?" Maria asked.

Danny frowned. "I think I swallowed something hard," he said.

"Swallowed it!" Maria cried, her eyes big with worry. She looked inside his mouth.

Teresa said, "I didn't bite into anything hard, but I think I'm sick." She held her stomach with both hands. Maria didn't dare look into Teresa's mouth!

She wanted to throw herself onto the floor and cry. The ring was now in her cousin's throat, or worse, his belly. How in the world could she tell her mother?

But I have to, she thought.

She could feel tears pressing to get out as she walked into the living room where the grown-ups sat talking.

They chattered so loudly that Maria didn't know how to interrupt. Finally she tugged on her mother's sleeve.

"What's the matter?" her mother asked. She took Maria's hand.

"I did something wrong," Maria sobbed.

"What?" her mother asked.

Maria thought about the beautiful ring that was now sitting inside Danny's belly, and got ready to confess.

Then she gasped. The ring was on her mother's finger, bright as ever.

"The ring!" Maria nearly screamed.

Maria's mother scraped off a flake of dried *masa*.

"You were playing with it?" she said, smiling gently.

"I wanted to wear it," Maria said, looking down at the rug. Then she told them all about how they'd eaten the tamales.

Her mother moved the ring a little on her finger. It winked a silvery light. Maria looked up and Aunt Rosa winked at her, too.

"Well, it looks like we all have to cook up another batch of tamales," Rosa said cheerfully.

Maria held her full stomach as everyone filed into the kitchen, joking and laughing. At first she still felt like crying as she kneaded a great bowl of *masa*, next to Aunt Rosa. As she pumped her hands up and down, a leftover tear fell from her eyelashes into the bowl and for just a second rested on her finger, sparkling like a jewel.

Then Rosa nudged her with her elbow and said, "Hey, *niña*, it's not so bad. Everyone knows that the second batch of tamales always tastes better than the first, right?"

When Dolores, Teresa, and Danny heard that from the other side of the room they let off a groan the size of twenty-four tamales.

Then Maria couldn't help herself: She laughed. And pretty soon everyone else was laughing, including her mother. And when Maria put her hands back into the bowl of *masa,* the leftover tear was gone.

Gary Soto

I am Mexican American, and I want to write stories that show my people and some of their traditions. In *Too Many Tamales*, I wanted to show the fun of making tamales at holiday time.

Would *you* like to be a writer? Then remember the things that happen in your life, good and not so good. You can put those things into your own stories someday.

Ed Martinez

Before I painted the pictures for *Too Many Tamales*, I took pictures of friends and other models. My wife and I made *many* tamales while working on the photographs. Then everyone got to eat them!

I used warm colors in my paintings to show the warmth of this family. The bright colors help show the family's Hispanic background.

I have my own warm family—my wife, Deborah, my little boy, Oliver, and a cat named Buckwheat.

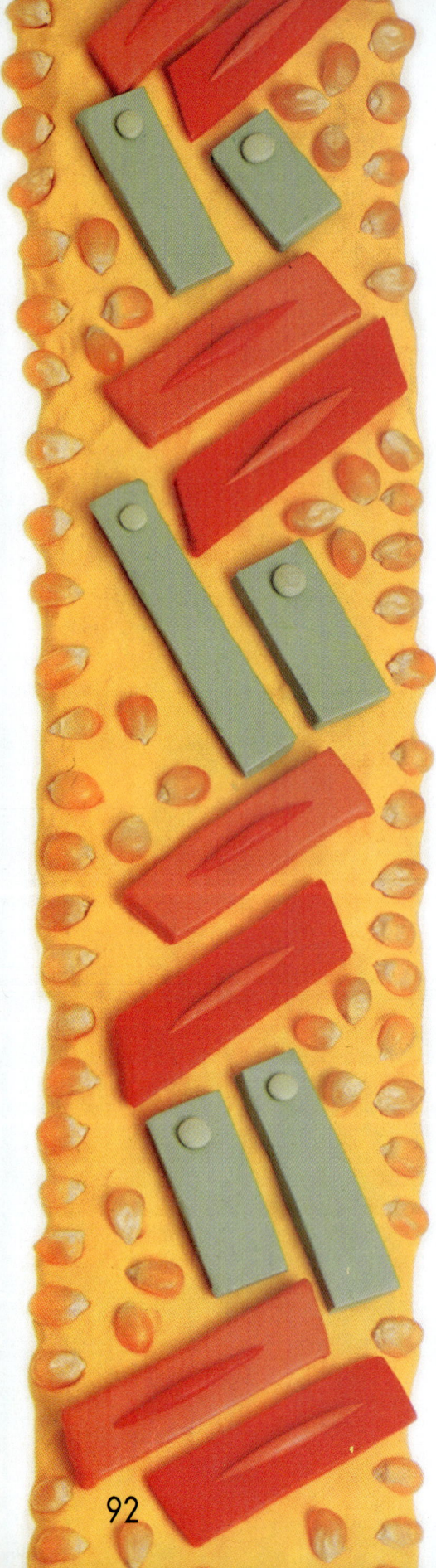

RESPONSE CORNER

FOLLOW A RECIPE

Cornmeal Fun Dough

Maria's family uses cornmeal to make tamales. You and your group can use cornmeal to make a special dough.

You will need:

bowl	1 ½ cups flour
measuring cups	1 ½ cups cornmeal
self-sealing plastic bag	1 cup salt
spoon	1 cup water

1. Stir together the flour, cornmeal, and salt.
2. Add water as you knead the dough with your hands.
3. Take turns kneading until the dough is "just right" (not too sticky).

When your dough is finished, you can use it to make different shapes. Store your dough in a plastic bag.

SOLVE A PROBLEM
Be a Problem Solver

Maria and her cousins ate all the tamales to try to find the missing ring. How would you have solved Maria's problem? Work with a group to find another way to solve Maria's problem.

1. Think about other things Maria could have done.
2. Choose your group's best idea.
3. Choose one person to share your group's idea with classmates.

What Do You Think?

- Why did Maria and her cousins eat all the tamales?
- Why do you think Maria didn't tell her mother when the ring was first missing?

A WORLD

Chinese people celebrate the new year on February 18. **Chinese New Year** starts off with a spring festival called **Chun Jie**. It is a time when parents and children clean and paint their homes. Everyone celebrates the new year with beautiful clothes and new shoes. The children's favorite part is eating lots of treats such as ice sticks.

Try this easy recipe and feel COOL!

You will need:
fruit juice, 1 small paper cup, tinfoil, 1 craft stick

1. Pour juice into a cup.
2. Cover the top with tinfoil.
3. Make a slit in the center of the foil. Put in the stick.
4. Freeze it.
   Now it's ready to eat!

OF TREATS!

Songkran is a festival to celebrate the new year in Thailand. The festival takes place in the middle of April, the hottest time of the year in Thailand. **Fruit leather** is a popular treat. Ripe fruit and a hot sun are all you need to make it!

You will need:
1 pound of strawberries or other pitless fruit, box, cheesecloth, blender, two plates, plastic wrap, pan
(Ask a grown-up to help you with steps 1 and 3.)
1. Mash the fruit in a blender.
2. Put the smooth fruit in a pan.
3. Cook on low heat until the fruit boils.
4. Turn off the stove, and let the pan cool.
5. Spread plastic wrap around each plate.
6. Spread the mashed fruit on each plate.
7. Put the plates in a box, and cover the box with cheesecloth. Then put the box in the sun. Your fruit leather will be ready to eat in 1 to 3 days.

Cinco de Mayo is Spanish for "May 5th." Cinco de Mayo is an important holiday for the people of Mexico. It is the day many years ago that Mexico became a free country. This holiday is also called Mexican Independence Day.

The Mexican children's favorite holiday treat is chocolate. Try this chocolate drink recipe, and sing the song as you stir your chocolate.

Uno - dos - tres **cho**	One - two - three **cho**
Uno - dos - tres **co**	One - two - three **co**
Uno - dos - tres **la**	One - two - three **la**
Uno - dos - tres **te**	One - two - three **te**
Cho - co - la - te	Cho - co - la - te
Bate, bate	Stir, stir
Cho - co - la - te	Cho - co - la - te

MEXICAN CHOCOLATE

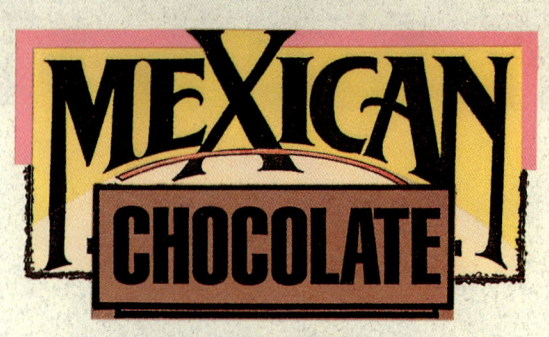

You will need:

1 ounce of chocolate powder (cocoa)

1 cup of cold water

a little honey

a little vanilla

Mix the ingredients in a glass, and stir with a spoon.

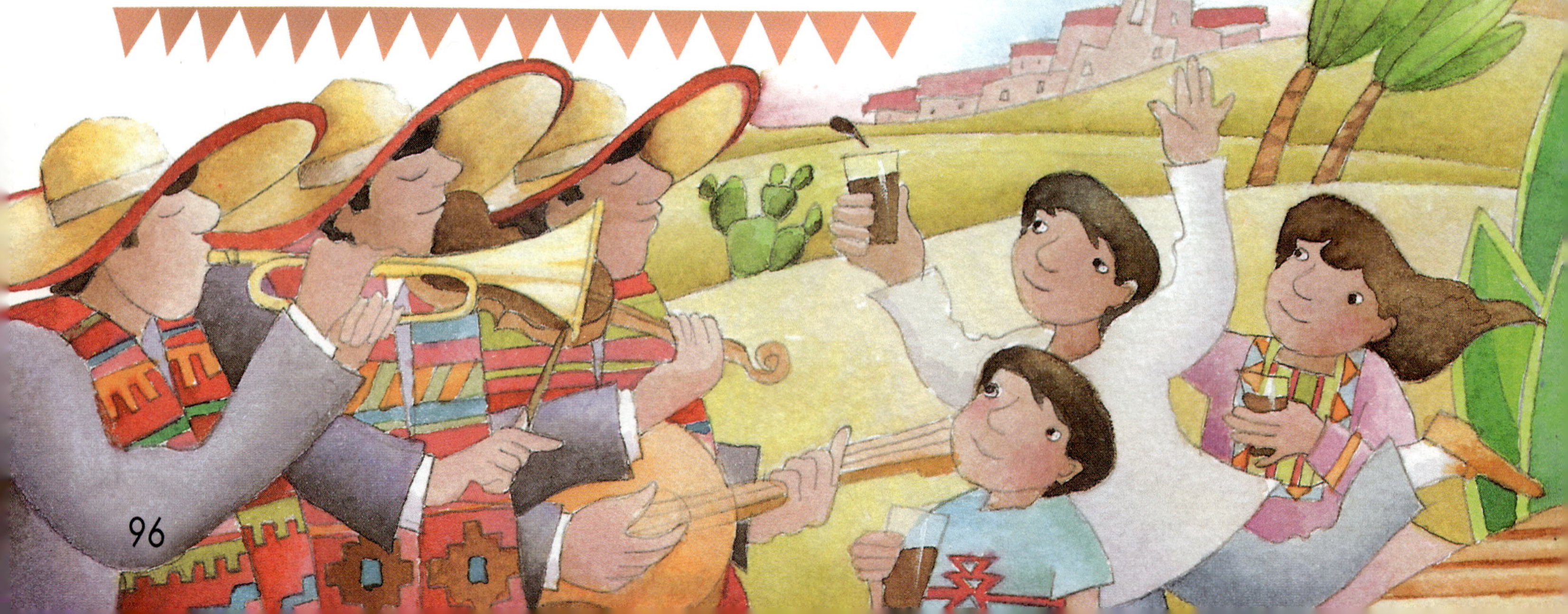

Birthdays are exciting for everyone! Kids like to have birthday parties so they can play games, get gifts, and eat treats and cake.

In the Philippines, kids celebrate birthdays in the same way. One of their favorite treats is sweet rice cakes. Try this sweet "sticky" treat, and have a **maligayang kaarawan!** ("Happy birthday!")

SUMAN
"SWEET RICE"

You will need:
1 can (about 2 cups) of sweetened coconut milk
2 cups of uncooked rice
sugar

(Let a grown-up help you with step 2.)

1. Put uncooked rice and coconut milk in a pot.
2. Cover the pot and cook the rice at medium heat for about 20 minutes.
3. Turn off the heat. Let the rice cool until it becomes a little stiff—about 10 minutes.
4. Shape 1 tablespoon of rice into a small square.
5. Sprinkle the top with sugar.

This recipe makes about 25 rice cakes.

Kwanzaa is an important time when African American families celebrate their heritage. The holiday begins on December 26 and ends on January 1. Every night until the first day of the new year, families light a candle. Also, they share a special drink from a cup called a **kikombe**.

Celebrate Kwanzaa! Make these holiday treats, and share them with your family and friends.

You will need:
sugar cookies,
  already baked
peanut butter
chopped peanuts

First, spread peanut butter on top of each cookie. Then, sprinkle with chopped peanuts.

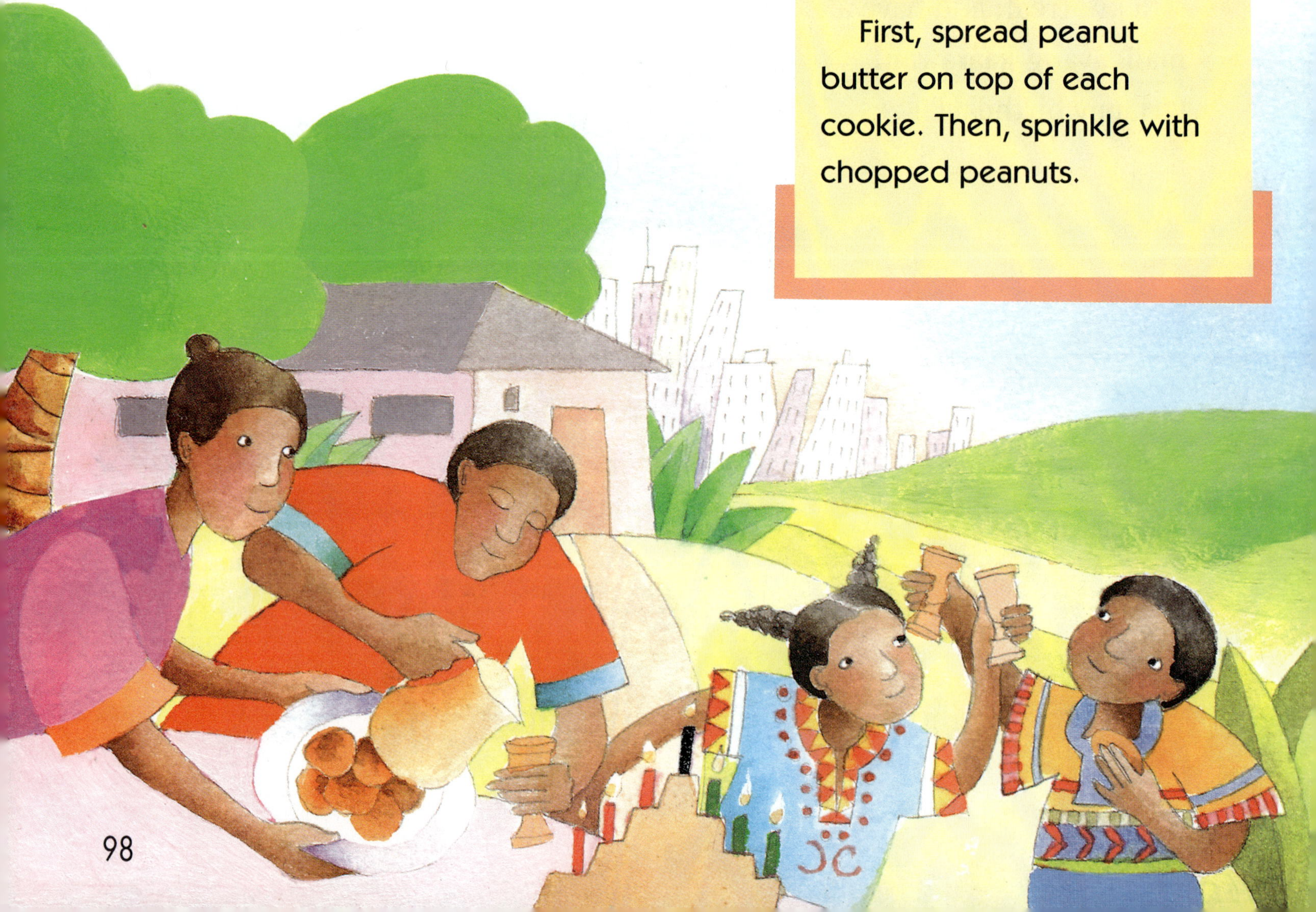

CARIBBEAN FRUIT PUNCH

You will need:
2 1/2 cups of lemonade
1 cup of orange juice
1 cup of pineapple juice
1 cup of papaya juice
1 cup of guava juice

Chill the juices. Then mix them together in a large bowl. After the juices have been mixed, pour the drink into your kikombe and enjoy! This recipe will make about 7 cups.

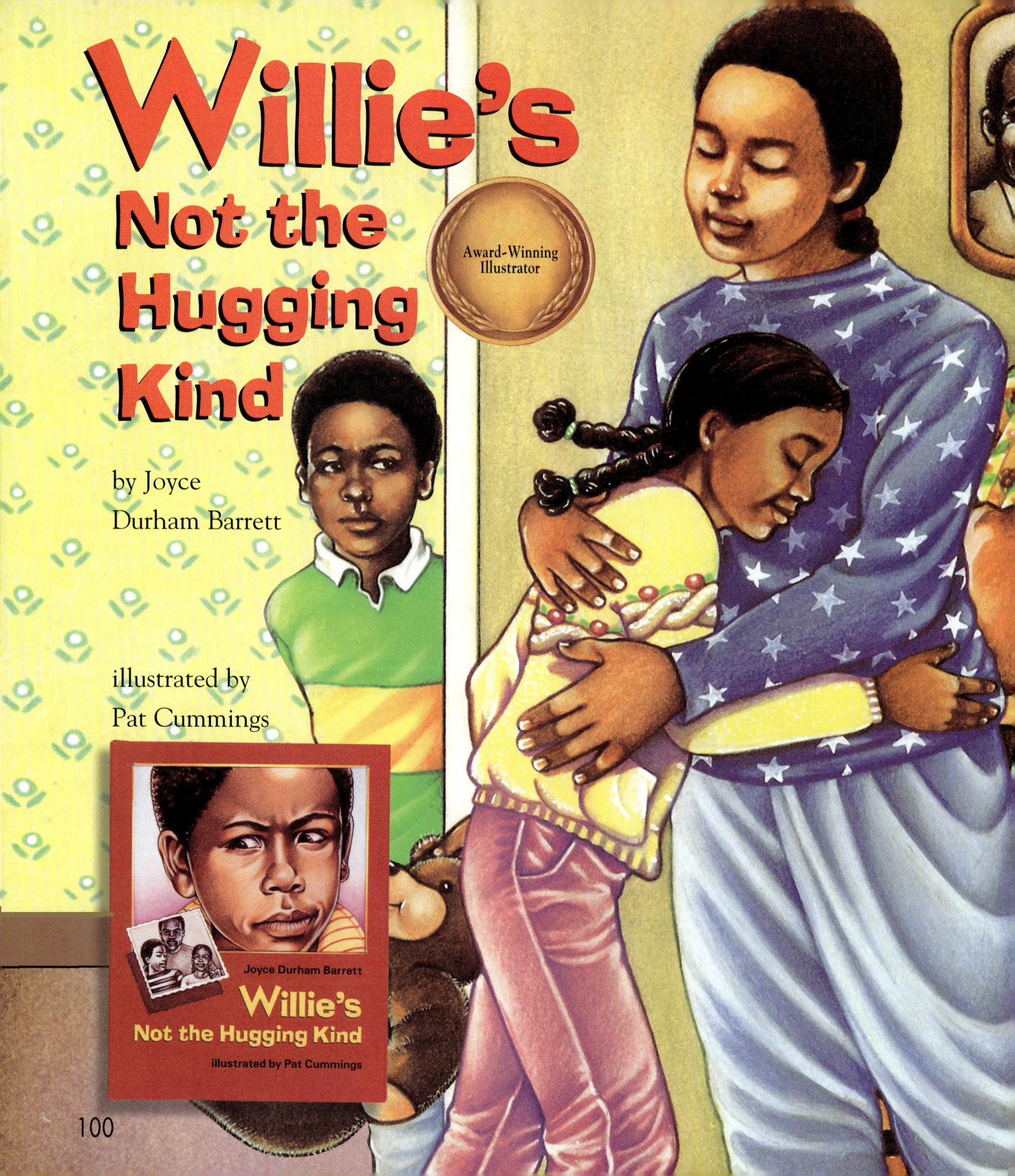

Willie wanted someone to hug. That's what he wanted more than anything.

But no one hugged Willie. Not anymore.

Not even his daddy when he dropped Willie and his friend Jo-Jo off at school. Now, he just patted Willie on the head and said, "See you around, Son."

Willie didn't like to be patted on the head. It made him feel like a little dog. Besides, hugging felt much nicer, no matter what Jo-Jo said.

Every day Jo-Jo rode to school in the linen truck with Willie and his daddy. And when Willie used to hug his daddy good-bye, Jo-Jo would turn his head and laugh. "What did you do that for? Man, that's silly," Jo-Jo would say once they had crawled out of the truck.

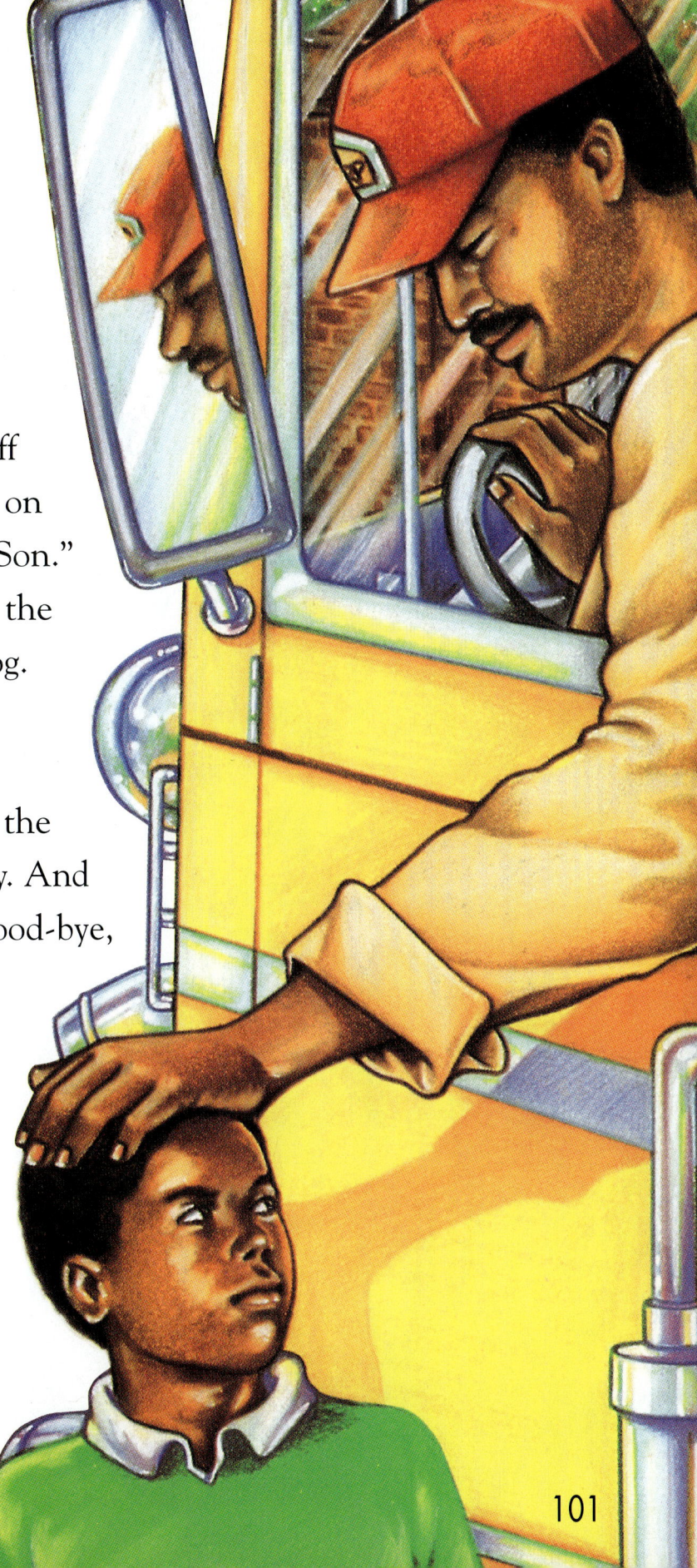

So Willie stopped hugging his daddy. He never hugged his mama or his sister anymore either.

And when they tried to hug Willie, he turned away. But Willie wanted someone to hug. That's what he wanted more than anything.

At school he watched as Miss Mary put her arms around some boy or girl. It didn't look silly. Except when she tried to hug Jo-Jo. Jo-Jo made a big commotion that made everyone laugh. He wriggled and squirmed, and shrieked, "Help! Help! I'm being mugged! Help!"

At night Willie watched his sister pull her teddy bear to her and hug it. She looked so safe and happy lying there with her arms around the bear.

"Why do you hug that old thing?" Willie said. "That's silly."

Rose frowned at Willie. "Who says?" she demanded.

"Jo-Jo says, that's who says," Willie boasted.

"Well, if you ask me, I think Jo-Jo's silly," said Rose. "Besides," she said, squeezing the bear to her, "Homer's nice."

But the next night Willie pinched his nose and said, "What a smelly old bear! I wouldn't hug that old thing for a hundred dollars. Not even for a million dollars. That's silly."

Rose pulled Homer in closer to her. "Willie," she said, "you're just not the hugging kind, then . . . if that's how you feel."

Willie flipped over in bed without even saying, "Good night, sleep tight, God keep you all right." And his mind went around and around on what his sister had said. The words tick-tocked back and forth with the clock sitting on the table by his bed:

NOT-the hugging kind,
NOT-the hugging kind,
NOT-the hugging kind,
if-THAT'S-how-you-feel.

But that was not how Willie felt. More than anything, Willie wanted to be the hugging kind.

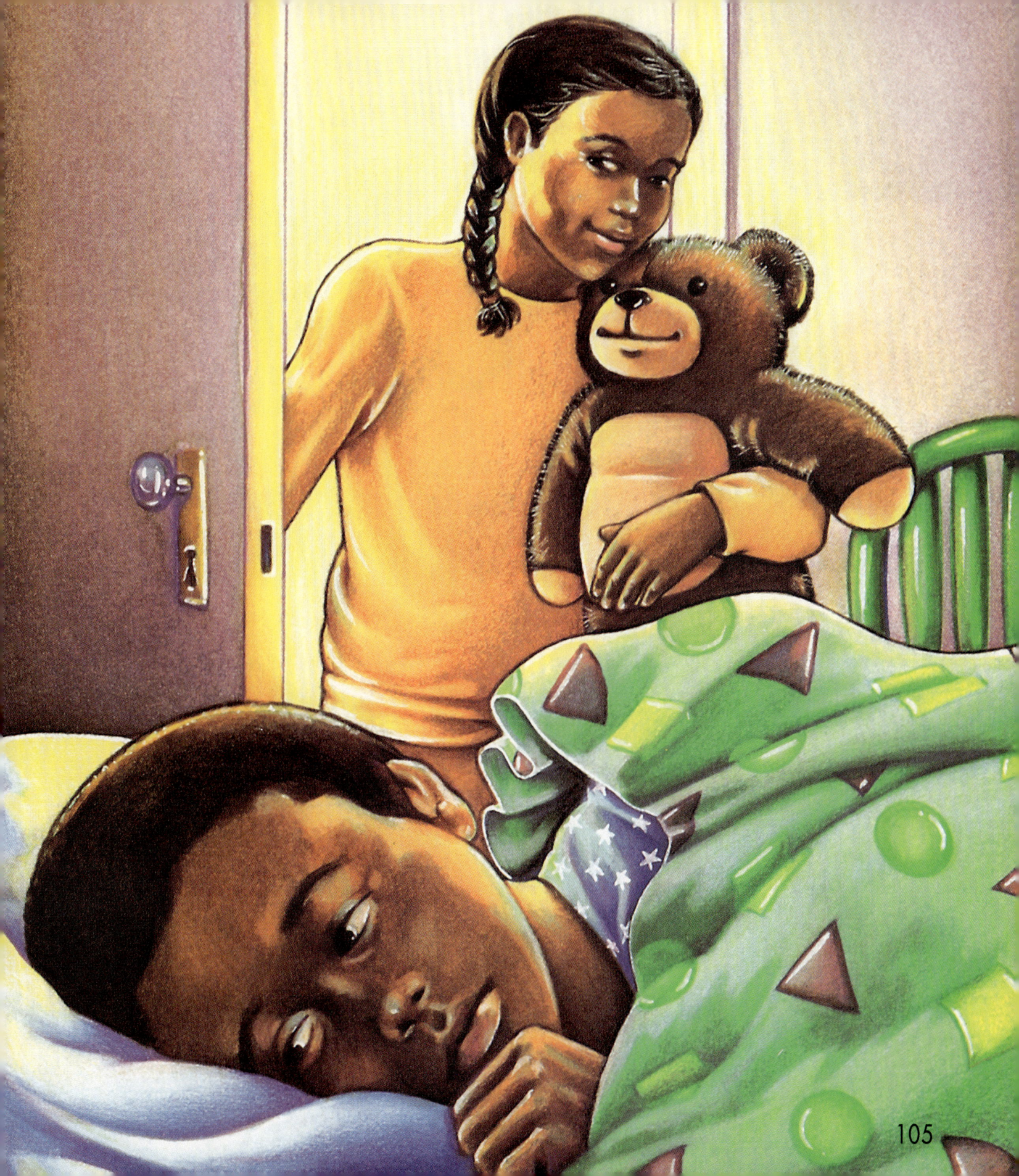

Willie watched each morning as his daddy hugged first his mama and then Rose. He remembered how safe and happy he always felt with his daddy's strong arms around him.

He remembered how good it felt to put his arms around his mama. She smelled a little like lemon and a little like the lilac powder in the bathroom. She felt big and a little lumpy. She also felt soft and safe and warm.

One morning Willie went into the kitchen and everyone was hugging everyone else. But no one hugged Willie. They didn't even see him. Willie waited, hoping someone would put their arms around him. If they did, maybe he wouldn't slip away.

But no one tried. Rose just said, when she saw Willie watching, "You know that Willie says he isn't the hugging kind now. He says it's all too, too silly."

"I did not!" said Willie, bristling. "Jo-Jo said that!"

"Oh, but you said it too, Little Brother," Rose said, laughing and tousling his hair.

Willie grabbed his lunch and his books, and ran out the door to meet Jo-Jo. "Let's get out of here!" Willie shrieked, breaking into a run. "They're mugging everybody in there!"

That afternoon Jo-Jo's mother picked him up after school, so Willie walked home alone.

He walked through the park and saw a young couple standing on the footbridge with their arms around each other.

He walked down Myrtle Street and saw a woman and a man rushing down the steps from their porch to greet some visitors with hugs all around.

It seemed so long since Willie had had a hug.

He walked into the long, low branches of a willow tree and wrapped his arms around it. A blue jay flew down from a purple plum tree, and Willie reached out to its fluttering wings. He walked up to a stop sign and hugged it.

He hugged his bike in the front yard. He hugged the door to his house when he opened it. And he rushed inside to hug his mama. But she was too busy running the vacuum over the floors. Willie was kind of glad. After all, he felt a little silly.

That night, after Willie had had his bath, he took the old bath towel and draped it across the head of his bed.

"What's that for?" Rose asked, hugging Homer to her.

"Nothing," said Willie.

The next night Willie put the old bath towel on the bed again. And the next night, and the next. Each night, when he was sure that Rose was not watching, he slipped the old towel down from the headboard and he hugged it. But it didn't feel soft and safe and warm.

Willie wanted to hug someONE, not someTHING.

In the morning Willie's mama was in the kitchen making biscuits. He watched Rose brush up to her and put her arms around her.

When the biscuits were finished and browning in the oven, Willie went up and put his arms around his mama too. Or almost around her. There was a little more to her than he remembered. She felt much nicer than an old towel. And, even better, she hugged back.

"What's all this, Willie," she said, "hugging around here on me so early in the morning?"

"Yeah, Willie," said Rose. "I thought all that hugging was too, too silly."

Willie clung tighter to his mama.

"That's all right," said his mama. "Willie knows, don't you, Son, that it's them that don't get hugging who think it's silly."

Willie looked up into his mama's face, smiling, until he felt a tap on his shoulder. Turning, he saw his daddy smiling down at him.

"My turn, Son," he said.

Willie put his arms around his daddy, burying his face in the familiar khaki shirt and feeling once again secure in the warmth of the strong arms around him.

Breakfast tasted better to Willie than it had in many a day. And when it came time to leave for school, Willie gave hugs all around.

Jumping into the big truck, Willie and his daddy stopped by to pick up Jo-Jo. When they arrived at school, Willie reached up and gave his daddy a quick, tight hug. Then he scooted out the door behind Jo-Jo.

"What did you do that for, man?" Jo-Jo said, once they were out of the truck. "Don't you know that's silly?"

Willie gave his friend a shove on the shoulder. Maybe Jo-Jo wouldn't let someone hug him, but he would allow a playful shove now and then. "Go on, now, Jo-Jo," he said. "I think *you're* what's silly."

Jo-Jo ran on ahead. "Help, help!" he shrieked. "I'm being mugged! Help!"

But Willie didn't mind. He lagged behind, feeling warm and safe knowing that he was, after all, the hugging kind.

Joyce Durham Barrett

Joyce Durham Barrett grew up with lots of people to hug. She was the tenth child in a family of eleven children. If each child hugged every brother and sister just once, how many hugs would that be? Barrett is a writer and a school teacher. She lives in Georgia with her daughter.

Joyce Durham Barrett

Pat Cummings

I don't always use real people in my pictures, but I did for this story. My husband posed for Willie's father, and a friend of mine posed for his mother. I had a hard time finding a Willie. Then I met a boy named David who was perfect for Willie. A friend of David's who came along with him posed for Jo-Jo.

I started by making sketches of how I wanted each picture to look. Then I had the real people pose like the sketches. I took photographs of them. I looked at the photographs as I painted the pictures.

The pictures you see in the story were first painted with watercolors on heavy paper. Then I went over them with colored pencil. You might like to try this on some of the pictures *you* paint!

Pat Cummings

MAKE A CARD

Send a HUG

You can send a hug through the mail if your hug is on a card!

 Fold a piece of paper in half. Cut it on the fold.

 Fold one of the strips into three equal parts.

 Draw an arm on the outside flap. Cut out a hand and glue it in place.

 Open the flap. Draw an arm on the next flap. Add a hand.

 Make a face that looks like yours. Cut it out and glue the head to the card.

 Write a special message inside the card.

RESPONSE

SHARE IDEAS

It's Not Easy

Willie learned that it's not easy to hug your dad when a friend says it's silly. What other things are not easy to do? Work in a group. Make a list of everyone's ideas. Choose one idea to share with your classmates. Plan a way to share your idea.

- You can make up a short play.
- You can draw a poster.

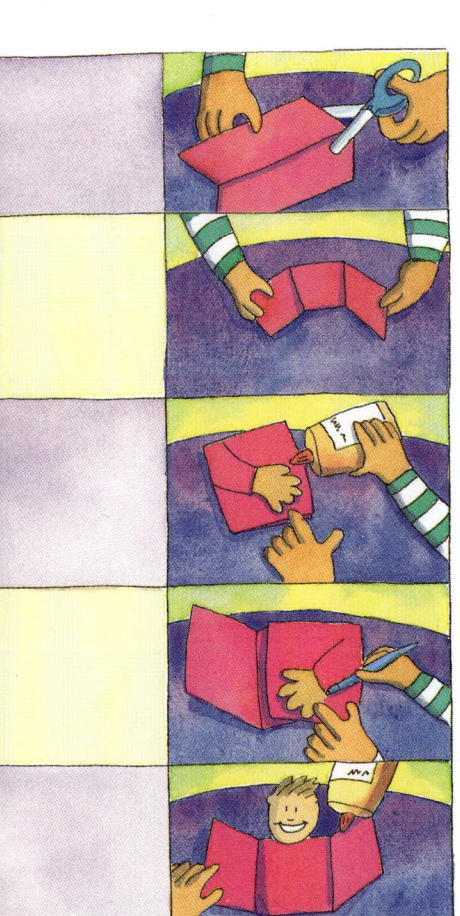

What Do You Think?

- Why did Willie let his family think he didn't like hugging?
- How did you feel at the end of this story? Why?

CORNER

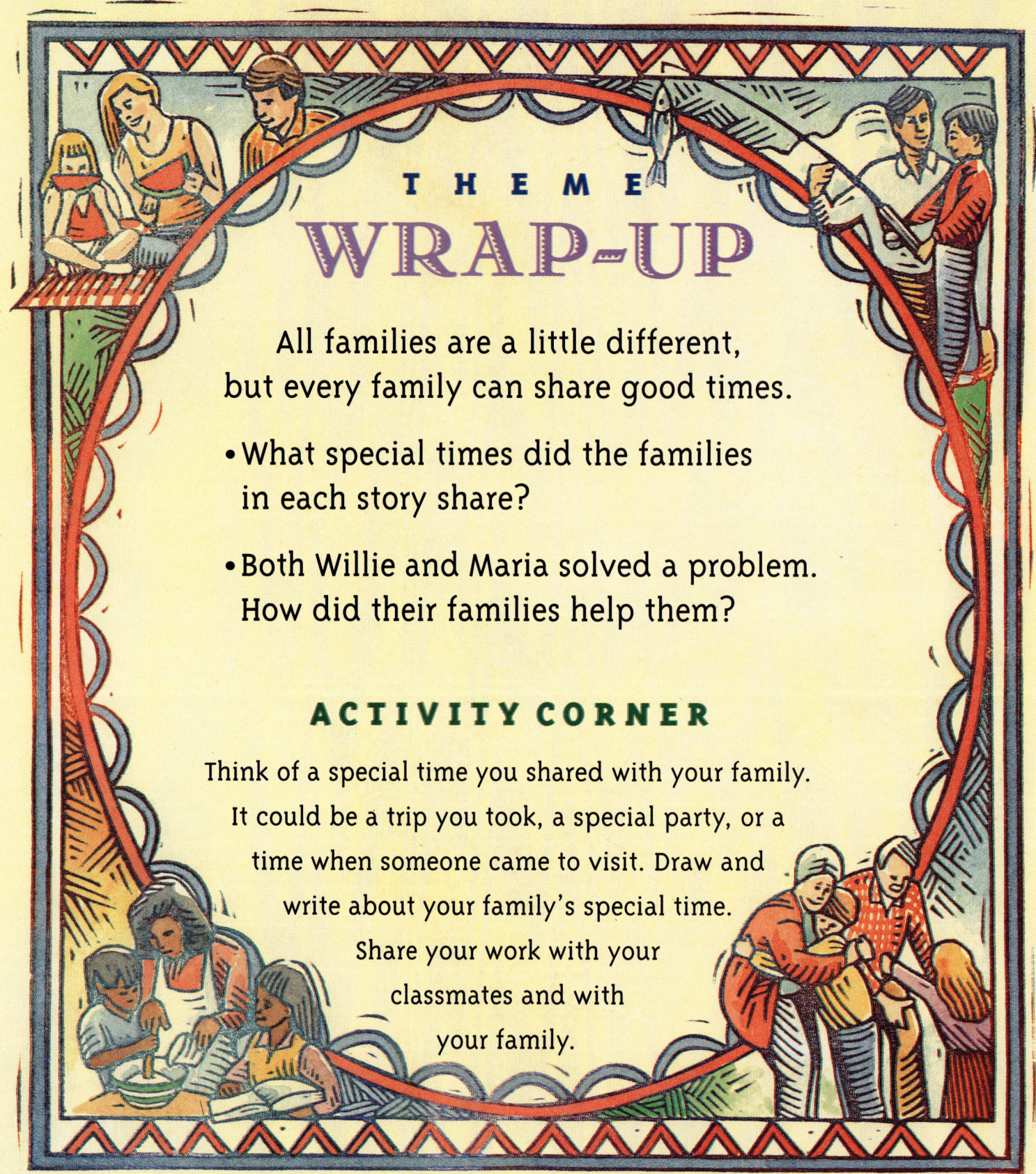

THEME WRAP-UP

All families are a little different, but every family can share good times.

- What special times did the families in each story share?

- Both Willie and Maria solved a problem. How did their families help them?

ACTIVITY CORNER

Think of a special time you shared with your family. It could be a trip you took, a special party, or a time when someone came to visit. Draw and write about your family's special time. Share your work with your classmates and with your family.

Using the Glossary

▶ Get to Know It!

The **Glossary** gives the meaning of a word as it is used in the story. It also has an example sentence to show how to use the word. A **synonym,** or word that has the same meaning, sometimes comes after the example sentence. The words in the **Glossary** are in ABC order, also called **alphabetical order.**

▶ How to Use It!

If you want to find *brilliant* in the **Glossary,** you should first find the **B** words. **B** is near the beginning of the alphabet, so the **B** words are near the beginning of the **Glossary.** Then you can use the guide words at the top of the page to help you find the entry word *brilliant*. It is on page 351.

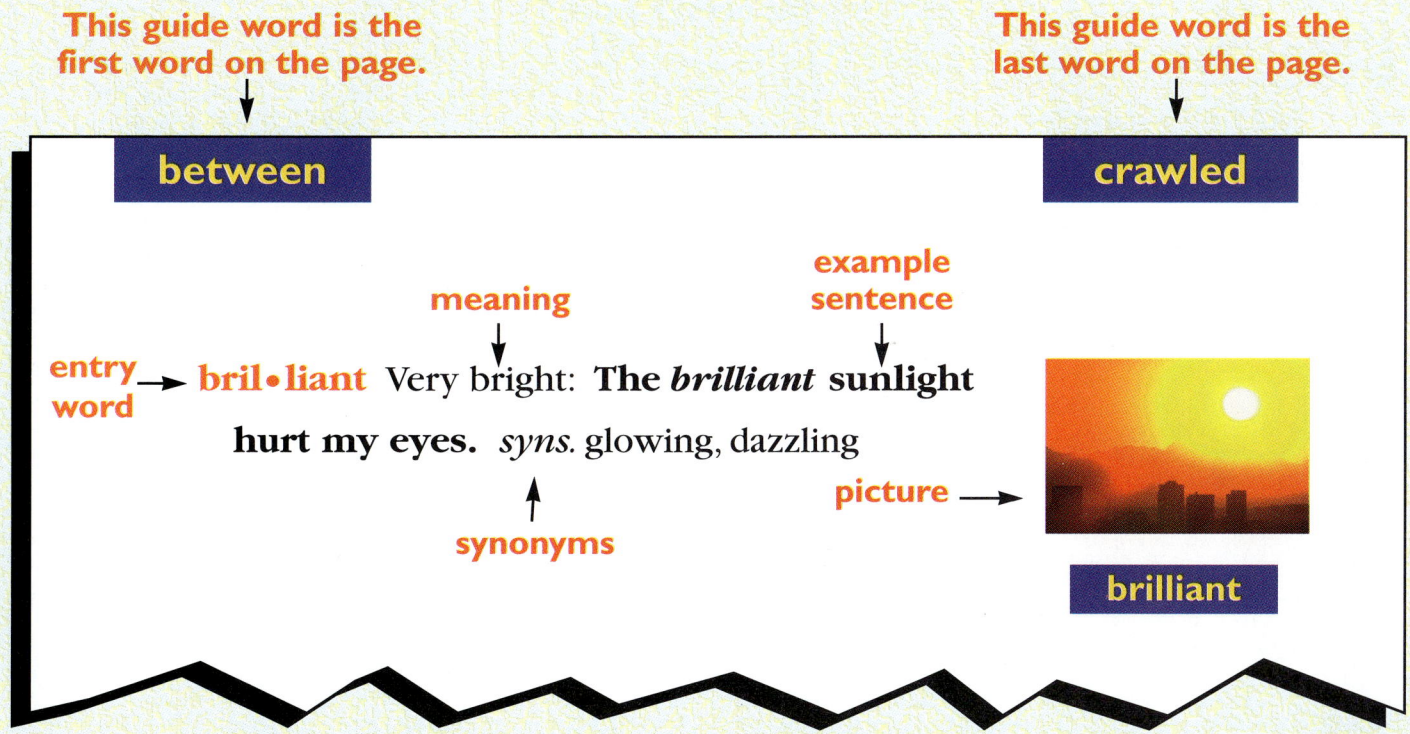

A

aboard

a•board Riding on things like ships, planes, and trains: **The people *aboard* the ship waved to the people back on land.**

ac•cept To put up with; to take: **Please *accept* this cake as my way of saying I'm sorry.**

ad•van•tage Something that helps one team do better than the other: **Our basketball players were taller, so we had the *advantage*.**

argue

al•read•y Before a certain time: **We have *already* eaten dinner, so we aren't hungry.**

an•nounced Told others: **She *announced* the winner of the contest.**

ar•gue To give reasons for or against something: **Sometimes my sister and I *argue* about who is right.** *syns.* disagree, fight

ar•gu•ment A fight with words: **Casey had an *argument* with his friend about who was faster.** *syns.* fight, quarrel

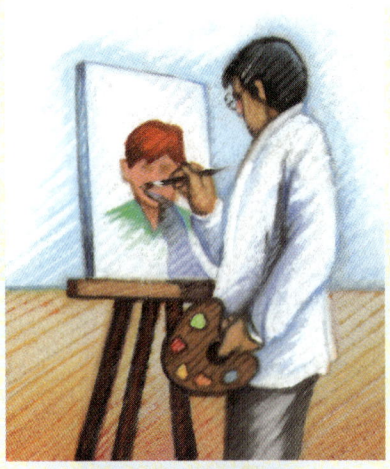
artist

art•ist A person who draws or paints: **The *artist* drew a picture of me.**

350

B

be•tween In the middle: **I sit *between* Simon and Isabel at school.**

blind•ing Making something hard to see: **The snow was so *blinding* that I couldn't see the house across the street.**

bril•liant Very bright: **The *brilliant* sunlight hurt my eyes.** *syns.* glowing, dazzling

brook A very small river: **Mom lets us play in the *brook* because the water is not deep.** *syn.* stream

bus•y Having a lot to do; working: **I was so *busy* doing my homework that I forgot my baseball practice.**

buy To use money to get something: **We *buy* food at the store.**

C

cou•ple Two people together: **The *couple* sat side by side on the bench.** *syn.* pair

cov•er To hide by moving in front of: **Clouds *cover* the sun in a storm.**

crawled Moved slowly: **The cars *crawled* along the crowded city street.**

brilliant

brook

couple

D

dan•ger•ous Not safe: **It can be *dangerous* to cross the street without first looking both ways.**

de•li•cious Tasting or smelling good: **I love the taste of those *delicious* cookies!** *syn.* tasty

de•light•ed Very happy: **I am *delighted* that you can come to my party.** *syn.* pleased

de•stroy To wreck; to ruin: **An earthquake can *destroy* a city.** *syn.* smash

dikes Walls to keep out water: ***Dikes* were built along the river to keep the water from flooding the town.**

dis•ap•pear To go away or become hidden: **We saw the train *disappear* into the tunnel.** *syn.* vanish

dough

dough Flour mixed with water and other things: **Uncle Ralph put the bread *dough* into a pan to bake.**

draw To make a picture: **Will you *draw* a horse for me?**

F

fair Giving everyone the same chance: **The game is *fair* because everyone has a chance to win.**

fam•i•ly A group of people who are related to one another: **My *family* and I eat breakfast together.**

fi•nal•ly At last; at the end: **Ben *finally* finished his story, one week after he started it.**

flood•ed Covered with water: **After it rained, people could not drive on the *flooded* streets.**

G

family

goes Leaves: **When the sun comes out, the snow *goes* away.**

grown Become larger: **Jake has *grown* two inches since last year.**

guide A person who shows others where to go: **A *guide* showed us the way to the monkey cages.**

H

hor•ri•ble Very bad: **The food tasted *horrible*, so he would not eat it.** *syn.* awful

hours Sixty minutes: **I'm in school for five *hours* each day.**

I

instrument

in•stru•ment Something you make music on: **Would you like to play an *instrument* in the band?**

J

jeans Strong cloth pants: **Maggie wore *jeans* to the school picnic.**

L

layers

larg•er Bigger: **My dad is *larger* than I am, so he wears bigger clothes.**

lay•ers Parts that lie one on top of the other: **The baker put icing between the *layers* of the cake.**

M

meadow

mead•ow A piece of land where grass grows: **We took the sheep to the *meadow* to eat the grass.** *syns.* field, pasture

min•ute Sixty seconds; a short amount of time: **I held the frog for a *minute* and then let it go.**

mouth•ful As much as can fit in a mouth: **Tomiko ate another *mouthful* of rice.**

music   **poem**

mu•sic Sounds you play on instruments or sing: **I like the *music* the band plays.**

N

new Not old: **Miguel got a *new* toy truck for his birthday.**

O

o•ceans Salt water that covers much of the earth: **Ships cross the *oceans* to go from one part of the world to another.** *syn.* seas

P

paintings

paint•ings Painted pictures: **Myra used red, yellow, and blue paints to make her *paintings*.**

pit•y A feeling of caring about someone who feels bad: **Peter felt *pity* for the boy who hurt his knee.**

plan•et A large, round body that goes around the sun: **The rocket flew around the *planet* Mars.**

po•em A group of sentences that often rhyme and that tell about thoughts and feelings: **Keneesha used the words hop, flop, and stop in her *poem* about a frog.**

planet

presents

pound•ed Hit very hard: **The man *pounded* the nail into the wood with a hammer.**

pres•ents Things people give to one another: **Kyle got many *presents* on his birthday.** *syn.* gifts

pro•duce To make: **That factory can *produce* many new cars each day.**

Q

quar•rel A fight: **They had a *quarrel* about who would ride the bike first.** *syn.* argument

R

real Not make-believe; not fake: **Rosa read a story about a castle and then visited a *real* one.**

rel•a•tives People in a family: **I like to visit Grandma, Grandpa, and my other *relatives*.**

re•plied Said something to answer a question: **Eddie *replied* "Yes" to the teacher's question.**

S

sea•son A certain time of year: **Summer is our hot *season*.**

se·cure Safe: **During the storm, we felt warm and *secure* in our house.**

shoul·der A part of the body, at the top of the arm: **Jan carried the bag over her *shoulder*.**

shove A hard push: **He gave the toy car a *shove* to start it rolling.**

show·er A short rain: **There was a light *shower* at the park, but I didn't get wet.**

shrieked Yelled in a high voice: **My aunt *shrieked* when the mouse ran across the floor.**

sil·ly Foolish; funny: **It would be *silly* to keep ice cream in a lunch box.**

slow·ly In a way that is not fast: **Kent was tired, so he walked *slowly* down the street.**

so·lar sys·tem The sun, the planets and their moons, and other things that go around the sun: **Jupiter is the largest planet in our *solar system*.**

squawked Made a loud noise like a parrot: **The bird *squawked* at us when we got too close.**

stom·achs More than one belly: **Our *stomachs* were full from dinner.**

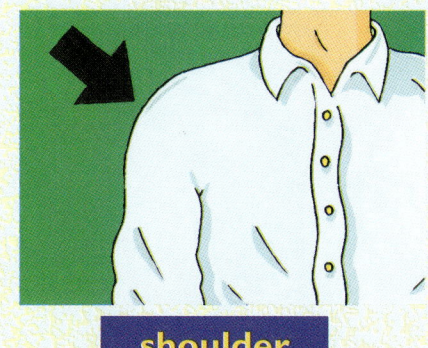

shoulder

shower

solar system

357

strange Not seen or heard of before: **We ate *strange* food when we went to a country far away.**

stretch•ing Growing: **The fog was *stretching* over the city.** *syn.* spreading

T

talk•ing Speaking: **The boys were *talking* to each other on the phone.**

tend To take care of: **Let's *tend* the garden so that the vegetables will grow.**

tend

thought Believed; felt: **Angie *thought* it was a beautiful day.**

through From beginning to end: **I read *through* the book without stopping.**

thun•der A loud noise made by lightning: **During the storm, we heard loud *thunder*.**

tour A trip to visit a place: **The class saw all kinds of animals on their *tour* of the zoo.**

U

underground

un•der•ground Below the ground: **We walked down steps to get on the *underground* train.**

V

vil•lage A small town: **Marco lives in a** *village* **near the top of a mountain.**

village

W

weath•er The way things are outside: **Do you like the cool** *weather* **in November?**

weighs Shows how heavy something is: **That heavy rock** *weighs* **fifty pounds.**

wom•en Girls who have grown up and now are adults: **Many** *women* **and men took care of the children.**

women

Copyright © 1997 by Harcourt Brace & Company

All rights reserved. No part of this publication may be reproduced or transmitted in any form or by any means, electronic or mechanical, including photocopy, recording, or any information storage and retrieval system, without permission in writing from the publisher.

Requests for permission to make copies of any part of the work should be mailed to: Permissions Department, Harcourt Brace & Company, 6277 Sea Harbor Drive, Orlando, Florida 32887-6777.

HARCOURT BRACE and Quill Design is a registered trademark of Harcourt Brace & Company.

Printed in the United States of America

Acknowledgments
For permission to reprint copyrighted material, grateful acknowledgment is made to the following sources:

Atheneum Books for Young Readers, an imprint of Simon & Schuster: Cover illustration by Ronald Himler from *Animals of the Night* by Merry Banks. Illustration copyright © 1990 by Ronald Himler.

Caroline House, Boyds Mills Press, Inc.: Cover illustration by Maryann Cocca-Leffler from *Wanda's Roses* by Pat Brisson. Illustration copyright © 1994 by Maryann Cocca-Leffler.

Children's Television Workshop, New York: "Family Treasure Chest" from *Kid City* Magazine, May 1994. Copyright 1994 by Children's Television Workshop. "Children of the Land" by Rhetta Aleong, illustration by Manuel King from *Kid City* Magazine, April 1995. Copyright 1995 by Children's Television Workshop.

Dial Books for Young Readers, a division of Penguin Books USA Inc.: Cover illustration by Carol Wright from *It Came from Outer Space* by Tony Bradman. Illustration copyright © 1992 by Carol Wright. *The Great Ball Game*, retold by Joseph Bruchac, illustrated by Susan L. Roth (adapted). Text copyright © 1994 by Joseph Bruchac; illustrations copyright © 1994 by Susan L. Roth. From *Batty Riddles* by Katy Hall and Lisa Eisenberg, illustrated by Nicole Rubel. Text copyright © 1993 by Katy Hall and Lisa Eisenberg; illustrations copyright © 1993 by Nicole Rubel.

Dutton Children's Books, a division of Penguin Books USA Inc.: Cover illustration by the Club de Madres Virgen del Carmen of Lima, Peru from *Tonight Is Carnaval* by Arthur Dorros. Illustration copyright © 1991 by Dutton Children's Books.

Greenwillow Books, a division of William Morrow & Company, Inc.: *Grandfather's Dream* by Holly Keller. Copyright © 1994 by Holly Keller. Cover illustration from *Tomorrow on Rocky Pond* by Lynn Reiser. Copyright © 1993 by Lynn Whisnant Reiser.

Harcourt Brace & Company: Cover illustration from *Stellaluna* by Janell Cannon. Copyright © 1993 by Janell Cannon.

HarperCollins Publishers: *Willie's Not the Hugging Kind* by Joyce Durham Barrett, illustrated by Pat Cummings. Text copyright © 1989 by Joyce Durham Barrett; illustrations copyright © 1989 by Pat Cummings. *Shooting Stars* by Franklyn M. Branley, illustrated by Holly Keller. Text copyright © 1989 by Franklyn M. Branley; illustrations copyright © 1989 by Holly Keller. "De Koven" from *Bronzeville Boys and Girls* by Gwendolyn Brooks. Text copyright © 1956 by Gwendolyn Brooks Blakely.

Holiday House, Inc.: *Postcards from Pluto: A Tour of the Solar System* by Loreen Leedy. Copyright © 1993 by Loreen Leedy. Cover illustration from *Who's Who in My Family?* by Loreen Leedy. Copyright © 1995 by Loreen Leedy.

Henry Holt and Company, Inc.: Cover illustration from *At the Beach* by Huy Voun Lee. Copyright © 1994 by Huy Voun Lee. *The Sun, the Wind and the Rain* by Lisa Westberg Peters, illustrated by Ted Rand. Text copyright © 1988 by Lisa Westberg Peters; illustrations copyright © 1988 by Ted Rand. Cover illustration by Margaret Hewitt from *Pearl Paints* by Abigail Thomas. Illustration copyright © 1994 by Margaret Hewitt.

Just Us Books Inc.: *Annie's Gifts* by Angela Shelf Medearis, illustrated by Anna Rich. Text copyright 1994 by Angela Shelf Medearis; illustrations copyright 1994 by Anna Rich.

Kane/Miller Book Publishers: *The Night of the Stars* by Douglas Gutiérrez, translated by Carmen Diana Dearden, illustrated by María Fernanda Oliver. Originally published in Venezuela in Spanish under the title *La Noche de Las Estrellas* by Ediciones Ekaré-Banco del Libro, 1987. Published in the United States by Kane/Miller Book Publishers, 1988.

Little, Brown and Company: "This Is My Rock" from *One at a Time* by David McCord. Text copyright 1929 by David McCord. Originally published in *The Saturday Review*.

National Geographic Society: From *Creatures of the Night* by Judith E. Rinard. Text copyright © 1977 by National Geographic Society.

Orchard Books, New York: *Shoes from Grandpa* by Mem Fox, illustrated by Patricia Mullins. Text copyright © 1989 by Mem Fox; illustrations copyright © 1989 by Patricia Mullins.

G. P. Putnam's Sons: *Too Many Tamales* by Gary Soto, illustrated by Ed Martinez. Text copyright © 1993 by Gary Soto; illustrations copyright © 1993 by Ed Martinez.

Scholastic Inc.: Cover illustration by J. Brian Pinkney from *Happy Birthday, Martin Luther King* by Jean Marzollo. Illustration copyright © 1993 by J. Brian Pinkney.

Simon & Schuster Books for Young Readers, a division of Simon & Schuster: *The Little Painter of Sabana Grande* by Patricia Maloney Markun, illustrated by Robert Casilla. Text copyright © 1993 by Patricia Maloney Markun; illustrations copyright © 1993 by Robert Casilla. Cover illustration by Cecily Lang from *A Birthday Basket for Tía* by Pat Mora. Illustration copyright © 1992 by Cecily Lang. *The Relatives Came* by Cynthia Rylant, illustrated by Stephen Gammell. Text copyright © 1985 by Cynthia Rylant; illustrations copyright ©1985 by Stephen Gammell. Cover illustration from *JoJo's Flying Side Kick* by Brian Pinkney. Copyright © 1995 by Brian Pinkney. Cover illustration by Roger Bollen from *Alistair in Outer Space* by Marilyn Sadler. Illustration copyright © 1984 by Roger Bollen.

Smithsonian Institution Press, Washington DC: Untitled poem (Retitled: "Rainbow Days") by Nootka, translated by Frances Densmore, from Bureau of American Ethnology, Bulletin #124.

Tambourine Books, a division of William Morrow & Company, Inc.: Cover illustration by James E. Ransome from *How Many Stars in the Sky?* by Lenny Hort. Illustration copyright © 1991 by James E. Ransome.

Ticknor & Fields Books for Young Readers, a Houghton Mifflin Company imprint: Cover illustration from *Ruth Law Thrills a Nation* by Don Brown. Copyright © 1993 by Don Brown.

Wordsong, Boyds Mills Press, Inc.: "Families, Families" by Dorothy Strickland and Michael Strickland from *Families*, selected by Dorothy S. Strickland and Michael R. Strickland. Text copyright © 1994 by Dorothy S. Strickland and Michael R. Strickland.

Photo Credits
Key: (t) top, (b) bottom, (c) center, (l) left, (r) right.
Hans & Judy Beste/ Animals Animals, 148(tl); Dennis Brack/Black Star/Harcourt Brace & Company, 141; Courtesy of Franklyn M. Branley, 190; Courtesy of Robert Casilla, 257(t); Steven Dalton/Animals Animals, 148(r)-149(l); Jack Dermid, 150(bl&r), 150(l); Courtesy of Ediciones Ekaré, 167(t), 167(b); Michael Greenlar/Black Star/Harcourt Brace & Company, 140; Harvard College Observatory/ Science Photo Library/ Phot Res. Inc., 178-179; Philip Hayson/ Photo Researchers, Inc., 182-183; Dale Higgins/Harcourt Brace & Company, 91(l); Joe Johnson III, 116; Ken Karp, 170-171, 314, 317; Russ Kinne, 146(r),147(l); Russ Kinne/ Comstock, 150(b); Ron Kunzman/Harcourt Brace & Company, 225; Wayne Lankinen/ Bruce Coleman, Inc., 150(tc); Tom McHugh/ Field Museum Chicago/ Photo Res. Inc., 185; NASA, 194-196, 198; Alan G. Nelson/ Animals Animals, 146(l); Pekka Parvianen/ Science Photo Library/ Photo Res. Inc., 174-175, 192-193; Carl Purcell/ Photo Res., Inc., 180-181; Rev. Ronald Royer/ Science Photo Library/ Photo Researchers, Inc., 186-187; Jerry Schad/Photo Researchers, Inc., 188-189; Flip Schulke/ Black Star, 288-289; Joe Sohm/ Photo Res., Inc., 184-185; Mark Souffer/Animals Animals, 151(tc); Tom Sobolik/Black Star/Harcourt Brace & Company, 91(r), 117, 191, 257(b), 345; Tony Star/ World Perspectives, 197; Superstock, 199; John Troha/Black Star/Harcourt Brace & Company, 256; Merlin D. Tuttle/ Photo Res. Inc., 149(br); Steve Woit, 312; Jacqui Wong 318-323; Photos from Cynthia Rylant's autobiography "Best Wishes" copyright © 1992 published by Richard C. Owens Publishers, Inc.; Edward Potthast *A Holiday* (1915), reprinted with permission from *Children's Book Press*, San Francisco, California, 68-69; Vincent van Gogh *The Starry Night* (1889), The Museum of Modern Art, New York, 172-173; Marc Chagall *The Green Violinist (Violoniste)*(1923-24), The Solomon R. Guggenheim Museum, New York, Photograph by David Heald © The Solomon R. Guggenheim Foundation, New York (FN 37.446), 286-287

Illustration Credits
Steve Johnson and Lou Fancher, Cover Art; Gyron Gin, 6-7, 13-17, 68-69, 120; Nathan Jarvis, 8-9, 121-125, 172-173, 228; Mercedes McDonald, 10-11, 229-233, 286-287, 348; Robert Casilla, 234-257; David Coulson, 194(t); Pat Cummings, 100-117; Stephen Gammell, 46-61; Iskra Johnson 174(t); Brenda Joysmith, 62-63; Kid City CTW, 68-69; Holly Keller, 174-191, 324-345; Loreen Leedy, 200-225; Ed Martínez, 70-91; Patricia Mullins, 18-43; María Fernanda Oliver, 152-167; Ted Rand, 290-313; Anna Rich, 262-283; Susan L. Roth, 126-141; Nicole Rubel, 142-143; Joanne Scribner, 168-169; Terry Widener, 258-259; Robert Casilla, 260-261; Pat Cummings 119(br); Susan Detrich, 64-65; Obadinah Heavner, 92-93; Jane Dill, 192-193; Ted Rand 316(t), 317(t&r); Loreen Leedy 226-227; Bonnie Matthews, 118-119; Rita Pocock Laskaro, 144-145; Lisa Pomerantz, 44-45; Anna Rich, 284-285; Scott Scheidly, 170-171, 284-285.